Sanskrit Poetics in the Postcolonial Space

Sanskrit Poetics in the Postcolonial Space

Beyond the Canon

Sreenath V.S.

B L O O M S B U R Y
NEW DELHI • LONDON • OXFORD • NEW YORK • SYDNEY

BLOOMSBURY INDIA
Bloomsbury Publishing India Pvt. Ltd
Second Floor, LSC Building No. 4, DDA Complex, Pocket C – 6 & 7,
Vasant Kunj, New Delhi, 110070

BLOOMSBURY, BLOOMSBURY ACADEMIC INDIA and the Diana logo are trademarks of Bloomsbury Publishing Plc

First published in India 2023
This edition published 2023

Bloomsbury Academic India
An imprint of Bloomsbury Publishing Plc

ISBN: HB: 978-93-56406-89-6; eBook: 978-93-56406-95-7
2 4 6 8 10 9 7 5 3 1

Typeset in Manipal Technologies Limited
Printed and bound in India by Replika Press Pvt. Ltd

Contents

Preface

Throughout its history of almost a millennium and a half, Sanskrit *kāvyaśāstra* was resolutely obsessed with the task of unravelling the ontology of *kāvya* (literary prose and poetry). Literary theoreticians in Sanskrit, irrespective of their spatiotemporal locations, unanimously agreed upon the fact that *kāvya* was a special mode of expression (distinctly different from the ordinary form of speech) characterised by the presence of certain unique linguistic elements. But, towards the turn of the 20th century, the Sanskrit *kāvyaśāstra* tradition underwent an epistemic rupture primarily because of a change in the way the idea of literariness was understood. During this phase, the traditional Formalistic notions about literature (to which Sanskrit *kāvyaśāstra* conformed) underwent a radical transformation, and the style and language of literature eventually became similar to everyday speech. This new trend severed Sanskrit *kāvyaśāstra*'s natural tie with literature. The mastery of Sanskrit poetics was no longer required to compose a literary work. Eventually, the vigour with which new treatises in Sanskrit poetics were produced also dwindled. This did not mean that the scholarship (*pāṇḍitya*) in Sanskrit poetics vanished. During this period, the focus of scholars in Sanskrit poetics slowly shifted from the production of new treatises in Sanskrit poetics to the creation of the intellectual history of this field.

During the postcolonial phase, especially in the 1980s, another attitudinal shift happened in studies on Sanskrit *kāvyaśāstra*. This shift, which can be labelled as a revivalist trend, once again aimed to use Sanskrit poetics—either in its original form or with necessary modifications—as an effective tool to evaluate the literary merit of modern Indian literary texts. This trend, which was spearheaded by Indian literary theoreticians such as K. Krishnamoorthy, Krishna

Rayan, Ayyappa Paniker, C.D. Narasimhaiah and so on, was the result of a strong desire to decolonise Indian literary criticism and introduce an alternative mode of criticism, that is modern, but not Western. Though this movement was lauded as a reassuring and promising move by many nativists, it failed to yield the desired effect. Why did this particular endeavour falter in maintaining its relevance? What is the politics of creating an alternative critical framework that is modern, but not Western? Do Sanskrit literary theories offer any new possibilities of research other than the ones offered by intellectual historiography and the revivalist attempts? These are the central questions that the book is going to grapple with in the forthcoming chapters. In this process, the book will also eventually examine the changes that this epistemology called Sanskrit poetics underwent during the colonial and postcolonial periods.

The book unfolds across five chapters. In Introduction, titled 'Mapping the Field', a nuanced conceptual dissection of the historical trajectory of Sanskrit *kāvyaśāstra* is undertaken. In the first chapter of this study, titled 'Beyond the Canon', the central argument of the work is presented. It asserts that the modern understanding of literariness has evolved significantly since the time of Sanskrit *kāvyaśāstra*. Literariness which was seen as an inherent characteristic of a text is now recognised as a dynamic construct generated by individual readers. This shift in perspective means that attempting to assess the artistic value of a work based on the traditional parameters set by Sanskrit *kāvyaśāstra* is inherently problematic. However, it is crucial to note that this does not diminish the importance of Sanskrit *kāvyaśāstra* as a field of study. In this chapter, I propose that instead of using Sanskrit *kāvyaśāstra* as a rigid benchmark for evaluating literary works or of limiting the focus of the study of *kāvyaśāstra* to the history of these concepts, the focus should also be on continually re-examining these theoretical concepts from fresh angles. This approach is akin to what Jacques Derrida calls 'play'. The next three chapters in the book demonstrates what I call 'play' vis-à-vis three concepts from Sanskrit poetics, namely *avivakṣita-vācya-dhvani*, *aucitya* and *vakrokti*.

The chapter on *avivakṣita-vācya-dhvani*, titled '*Avivakṣita-vācya-dhvani* and the Restructuring of Conventional Semantic Ambit' makes a non-canonical reading of the *avivakṣita-vācya*-variety of *dhvani* conceptualised by the 9th-century Sanskrit literary critic Ānandavardhana in his seminal work *Dhvanyāloka*. Here, I argue that *avivakṣita-vācya-dhvani*, through a process of deterritorialisation, opens up a signifier to new significations that are not conventionally associated with it. In any language, convention functions as a structuring mechanism upon a signifier by clearly demarcating a rigid semantic ambit for it. It is precisely this structuring tendency of the convention that gets challenged in Ānanda's *avivakṣita-vācya-dhvani*. Such a mechanism is definitely a liberating experience for both the signifier and the individual users (both the author and the reader or speaker and listener) of language who are otherwise forced to accept the signifiers in a specific fashion. Along with the exposition of *avivakṣita-vācya-dhvani*'s resistance to a signifier's conventional semantic ambit, this chapter also aims to conceptualise the figure of the reader that *avivakṣita-vācya-dhvani* anticipates for itself.

The third chapter, titled '*Aucitya*: A Mechanism of Control', deals with the concept of *aucitya* which was central to the Sanskrit *kāvyaśāstra* tradition throughout its history. Here, I argue that the concept of *aucitya*, propagated and practised by the Sanskrit literary theoreticians from Bharata to Jagannātha, can also be seen as a political tool to socially and aesthetically condition the predominantly upper-class, upper-caste male readers of Sanskrit *kāvya* in close conformity with the dominant power-structure of the society. This social and aesthetic conditioning that *aucitya* performed acted upon the reader through three inter-connected levels, starting with the Sanskrit literary theoreticians conditioning the creative writer, then the creative writer conditioning the creative artefact and finally the creative artefact conditioning the reader.

The fourth chapter, titled '*Vakrokti* as a Resistance to *Svabhāva*', deals with the idea of *vakrokti* (figurative deviation of utterance) as conceptualised by the 10th-century Sanskrit literary critic Kuntaka in his seminal work *Vakroktijīvita*. In this chapter, I delve into Kuntaka's notion of *vakrokti* as a form of creative expression aimed at broadening the imaginative horizons of both the author and the reader. This is achieved by guiding them away from their usual patterns of performance and perception, ultimately enhancing their shared range of experiences. As opposed to the infinite enactment of the same old structures which results in a restricted form of thinking and acting, Kuntaka's theory of *vakrokti* creates immense possibilities to experiment with the existing structures, both linguistic and non-linguistic. As far as Kuntaka is concerned, the act of depicting the nature of things in the way they appear to us (*svabhāvokti*) is not the job of a poet (*kavi*). His philosophy of literature, I argue, sees *kāvya* as a transformative or 'creative' act which aims to shatter the readers' ontological certitude about the ideas and entities in the world they live in.

The concluding chapter of the book emphasises the importance of challenging received notions about a text and adopting a sense of critical irreverence in order to facilitate the growth and evolution of any knowledge system, whether it is in a modern or ancient context. This spirit of relentless inquiry and questioning was the very lifeblood of Sanskrit *kāvyaśāstra* until it encountered a notable decline in creative vigour in the era marked by colonialism. In this context, I problematise the plausible reasons as to why we are reluctant to exercise a sense of dissent with respect to the classical systems of knowledge from early India. The book is brought to an end in an open-ended fashion, advocating for a continued 'play' with not only Sanskrit *kāvyaśāstra*, but with all knowledge systems, classical or modern. The goal is to view these systems as dynamic and ever-evolving entities, rather than as static and rigid constructs. The book aims to invite readers to join on an intellectual odyssey, where the pursuit of knowledge is marked by curiosity, scepticism and a fearless spirit of inquiry.

Acknowledgements

Sanskrit *kāvyaśāstra* has held an enduring fascination for me ever since I first encountered Bharata's *Nāṭyaśāstra* during my undergraduate days. I can unequivocally state that my passion for this field of knowledge has remained unwavering over the years. Whenever I delve into the texts of this rich tradition, I am struck by the vast expanse that remains unexplored, leaving me with the realisation that a single lifetime is insufficient to fully grasp its profound depths.

In my quest to comprehend this epistemology, Dr Mini Chandran at IIT, Kanpur has been an invaluable pillar of support. Her meticulous guidance, scholarly insights and unwavering dedication to the literary traditions of early and medieval India have played a pivotal role in shaping my ideas into a coherent body of knowledge. Through her astute suggestions and constructive criticisms, she has been instrumental in transforming my thoughts into a well-organised scholarly work. Moreover, our discussions on the viability and relevance of traditional epistemologies in the contemporary world have profoundly altered my perspectives on how we should approach and apply knowledge systems from the past.

I am deeply indebted to my Sanskrit teachers, Meenakshi Bapat and Amit Rao, who initiated me into the intricacies of the Sanskrit language and generously extended their assistance whenever I required it. Prof. Sheldon Pollock at Columbia University and Prof. Yigal Bronner at the Hebrew University of Jerusalem graciously responded to my inquiries via email and provided valuable reading materials from their personal collections. Their unwavering dedication to their work, their resilience and their profound love for knowledge have been a constant source of motivation.

I would also like to extend my heartfelt gratitude to my spouse and esteemed colleague, Dr Anandita Pan. Her unwavering support and insightful inquiries have been instrumental in refining my ideas and enhancing the quality of this thesis. Our shared research interests, mutual encouragement and in-depth discussions on topics within our respective fields of study have undeniably fuelled our motivation and served as a constant source of inspiration for both of us.

I am deeply grateful to *South Asian Review* (Taylor and Francis), *Journal of Indian Philosophy* (Springer), *Indian Literature* (Sahitya Akademi) and *Economic and Political Weekly* for their generosity in granting me the necessary permissions to reproduce select portions of this book.

Introduction: Mapping the Field

The Four Phases of Sanskrit Poetics

Śāstra or the prescription of acceptable practices in a field of knowledge was an integral part of almost all knowledge systems in early and medieval India, covering a wide range of areas such as ethics and morality (*dharmaśāstra*), sex (*kāmaśāstra*), drama (*nāṭyaśāstra*), sculpture (*śilpaśāstra*), astrology (*jyotiśāstra*) and salvation (*mokṣaśāstra*). According to Patrick Olivelle, the term *śāstra* 'signifies both a discipline and a treatise'. It is simultaneously 'a system of knowledge that a person would seek to master and a treatise codifying such knowledge that a person would read, memorize and understand' (2017: 13). Codifying 'the positive and negative regulation of some given human practice', *śāstra* in any discipline played a vital role in preventing any aberration in the praxis of knowledge (Pollock 1985: 501). In the realm of *kāvya*, the beginning of the *śāstra* tradition can be traced back to the 7th century. Since then, till around the beginning of colonialism in the 17th century, *kāvyaśāstra* played a vital role in defining the form and shape of literature in what Pollock calls the 'Sanskrit cosmopolis'.[1] Though the direct influence of Sanskrit poetics upon literary productions in the former 'Sanskrit cosmopolis' waned over the subsequent centuries due to Western literary influences, it continued to endure in the discussions of native critics both as a high watermark of India's contribution to literary criticism and as a powerful nativist instrument to decolonise Indian critics. Drawing on the nature of the *kāvyaśāstra* tradition and the attitude of critics and creative writers towards it, the Sanskrit *kāvyaśāstra* tradition from its beginning in the 7th century to date can be broadly divided into four phases namely 'the early phase' (7th–12th century), 'the medieval phase' (13th–17th century), 'the reconstructionist and the disseminationist phase' (17th century–1984) and 'the revivalist phase' (1984–to date).

Before analysing the characteristics of these four phases and tracing the evolution of Sanskrit *kāvyaśāstra* over the centuries, it is important to reflect upon the two key terms, namely Sanskrit and *kāvya* which define the discursive boundaries of the *kāvyaśāstra* tradition. While Sanskrit is the language in which these treatises on poetics are written, *kāvya* is the topic of their discussion.

Before the Common Era, Sanskrit was exclusively an idiom of Vedic rituals and other allied scholastic disciplines. While Sanskrit remained a language of *dharma*, Prākrit was the language of mundane affairs. It was only by the beginning of the Common Era that Sanskrit entered, rather gradually and hesitantly, into the public realm for worldly communicative practices like *kāvya* (Pollock 2003: 62). We have a slew of texts from the Vedic period which vindicate this observation. For instance, Patañjali, the great commentator of Pāṇini's *Aṣṭādhyāyī* (4th century BCE), sees no scope for Sanskrit studies outside the framework of the Vedic realm. All the five functions of learning Sanskrit that Patañjali enumerates in his *Mahābhāṣya* (2nd century BCE) are oriented towards perfecting one's knowledge of Vedic scriptures. These five functions of Sanskrit that Patañjali mentions include *rakṣa* (the process of preserving the Vedic message in language), *ūhā* (the act of re-contextualising the Vedic passage through linguistic analysis), *āgama* (the praxis of Scriptural injunctions), *laghu* (reduction of the effort required for understanding the complex passages in the *Veda*) and *asaṃdeha* (the removal of doubts regarding the interpretation of scriptural prescriptions) (Patañjali 1986: 26). Patañjali's reference to the Yarvāṇastārvāṇa sages further shows that the requirement of using Sanskrit was limited to the Vedic domain. These sages were nicknamed Yarvāṇastārvāṇa precisely because they used to code-switch between Sanskrit and Prākrit, based on what the occasion demanded. While these sages reserved the Sanskrit *yad vā naḥ, tad vā naḥ* for Vedic rituals, they used its non-standard Prakritic form—*yarvāṇas tārvāṇaḥ*—outside the Vedic realm, thereby preserving Sanskrit for the *vaidika* affairs and Prākrit for the mundane business. Patañjali observes, 'There were *ṛṣi*s [nick-]named Yarvāṇastārvāṇa . . . These worthy persons used [the expression] *yarvāṇas tārvāṇaḥ*, when they should have used *yad vā naḥ, tad vā naḥ*, "whatever (happens) to us, (let) that (happen) to us." But they did not use incorrect words at the time of sacrificial ritual' (156).

Before the Common Era, even Buddhists, who later produced a lot of works in Sanskrit, consciously stayed away from communicating their ideas in Sanskrit. Buddha's outright rejection of his disciple's plea to propagate the Buddhist teachings in Sanskrit bears testimony to it. *Vinayapiṭaka*, which was written in Pāli sometime between the 4th and 5th centuries BCE, records Buddha's words to his disciples.

> Two monks, Brahmins by birth, of fine language and fine speech, came to Buddha and said: Lord, here monks of miscellaneous origin are corrupting the Buddha's words by repeating them in their own dialects; Let us put them into Vedic [Sanskrit]. The Lord Buddha rebuked them: Deluded men, how can you say this? This will not lead to the conversion of the converted . . . And he delivered a sermon and commanded the monks: You are not to put Buddha's words into Vedic [Sanskrit]. Who does so would commit a sin. I authorize you, monks, to learn Buddha's words each in his own dialect. (quoted in Edgerton 1953: 139)

The situation remained unchanged even when Aśoka (320–150 BCE), the third emperor of the Maurya dynasty, introduced the technique of writing for the public promulgation of his edicts (*śāsana*). Aśoka's inscriptions, other than the ones composed in Greek and Aramaic, were mostly written in the local languages, especially Prākrit (Thapar 2002: 182).

It was only by the beginning of the 1st millennium BCE that Sanskrit started making its appearance in the public domain through some inscriptions. However, the amount of Sanskrit used in these inscriptions was 'by and large exiguous: one-or two-line records commemorating a *vaidika* or quasi-*vaidika* rite' (Pollock 2006: 60). Sanskrit, in fact, had to wait as late as the 2nd century to make its presence prominently felt in the public realm. According to the available historical evidence, the first major non-Vedic employment of standard Sanskrit was found in the Junagarh inscription (150 CE) from what we now call Gujarat.[2] Composed by the Western Kṣatrapa ruler Rudradāman to mark the reconstruction of a great water reservoir named Sudarśana which was heavily damaged in a storm, the Junagarh inscription is the first long inscription recorded entirely in more or less standard Sanskrit, as well as the first extensive record in the poetic style (1998: 89).[3] Close on the heels of Sanskrit's emergence outside the closet of the Vedic realm is the beginning of the *kāvya* tradition in Sanskrit. The maximum outer limit that we can set for the beginning of the *kāvya* tradition is the last centuries before the advent of the Common Era. 'From among the vast library of early Sanskrit texts,' says Pollock, 'no evidence compels belief in the existence of *kāvya* before the last centuries B.C.E., if that early' (2003: 84). Creative writers and literary critics from Sanskrit literary culture consider Vālmīki's *Rāmāyaṇa* as the first *kāvya* (*ādikāvya*) in Sanskrit. According to Pollock, the plausible reason for considering the *Rāmāyaṇa* as *ādikāvya* 'may have to do with its relationship to writing' (87). He observes that the *Rāmāyaṇa* was probably the first major text 'to be preserved, if not composed, in written form' (87).

The Beginning of *Kāvyaśāstra* Tradition

Although *kāvya* originated as early as the beginning of the Common Era, attempts to systematise the knowledge about the art of composing *kāvya* began only in the 7th century with Bhāmaha's *Kāvyālaṅkāra*, the earliest available text in the *kāvyaśāstra* tradition. This does not imply that prior to Bhāmaha, there were no discussions about *kāvya*. The case must have been such that the deliberations about the art of composing poems might have been conducted orally by poets and lay connoisseurs of verbal art without collating their ideas into a systematic body of knowledge (Bronner 2016: 84–85).[4]

At this juncture, it is also important to draw a distinction between *nāṭyaśāstra* and *kāvyaśāstra.* In Sanskritic cultural history, the term poetics in its broadest sense was concerned with two subject matters, namely *nāṭya* and *kāvya.* The factors that distinguished *nāṭya* from *kāvya* in terms of style, composition and aesthetic effect were so strong that Sanskrit poetics virtually got bifurcated into two streams such as *nāṭyaśāstra* and *kāvyaśāstra* (Gerow 1977: 223).[5] While the *nāṭyaśāstra* tradition of poetics focused primarily on the performance of drama on stage with the accompaniment of *āṅgika, vācika, āhārya* and *sāttvika* modes of acting [*abhinayas*],[6] *kāvyaśāstra* was exclusively concerned with the ontology of *kāvya* (poetry and literary prose).[7] Although texts in the *nāṭyaśāstra* tradition such as Bharata's *Nāṭyaśāstra* later exercised a veritable influence upon *kāvyaśāstra*, especially through the understanding of how literature embodies *rasa* (aesthetic emotion), its focus was primarily the structure of drama in performance, not the theory of literature (Pollock 2003: 42).[8]

Even though Bhāmaha's *Kāvyālaṅkāra* inaugurated Sanskrit poetics and very much served as a guiding light for the subsequent literary theoreticians, it was Daṇḍin's *Kāvyādarśa* (7th century) that became heavily influential for various non-Sanskritic literary traditions. Throughout the Sanskrit cosmopolis, this work was thoroughly studied and readapted. *Siyabaslakara* (9th century) in Sinhala, *Taṇṭiyalaṅkāra* (10th century) in Tamil, Sangharakṣita's *Subodhālaṅkāra* (12th century) in Pāli, etc., are a few vernacular treatises on poetics, based on Daṇḍin's *Kāvyādarśa* (Pollock 2006: 163). According to Pollock, 'All these make Daṇḍin's *Mirror* [*Kāvyādarśa*] the most influential work on literary science in world history after Aristotle's Poetics' (163).

Kāvyaśāstra or literary theory, as it was practised in Sanskrit cosmopolis, was essentially an attempt to understand the formal features that constitute 'literariness' in *kāvya*. It is believed that it was the presence of certain special linguistic features such as poetic suggestion, figures of speech, figurative deviation, etc., that attributed literariness to a work of art. Therefore, throughout its history of almost a millennium, Sanskrit *kāvyaśāstra* was exclusively preoccupied with the task of identifying and analysing the formal devices generating literariness in a work of art. Considering *kāvya* as a 'special' and 'specialized' mode of language marked by the 'ingenious' use of certain distinctive linguistic devices, *kāvyaśāstra* always made it a point to delimit *kāvya* from other uses of language such as *śāstra*, the *Veda*s and workaday language. Literary theoreticians in Sanskrit, irrespective of their spatiotemporal locations, unanimously agreed that *kāvya* was a special mode of expression (distinctly different from the ordinary form of speech), characterised by the presence of certain unique linguistic elements. Nonetheless, this did not imply that *kāvyaśāstra* was an intellectual tradition unmarked by disagreements. The most important and long-standing of all the points of contention among the practitioners of Sanskrit literary theory was the prioritisation of certain formal elements as the 'soul' of literature. This strong sense of intellectual disagreement on the question of what constituted the 'soul' of *kāvya* eventually paved the way for the emergence of new frameworks of criticism and an in-depth analysis of various formal elements, thus playing a vital role in keeping this tradition alive and active.

Among the various centres of Sanskrit scholarship, what rose to fame as the prime locus of the production of Sanskrit literary theories in the early period was undoubtedly the place which we now call Kashmir. A few names that mark the prominence of Kashmir in the intellectual history of Sanskrit *kāvyaśāstra* include Bhāmaha (7th century), Vāmana (9th century), Udbhaṭa (9th century), Ānandavardhana (9th century), Rudraṭa (9th century), Pratihārendurāja (9th century), Mukula Bhaṭṭa (9th century), Kuntaka (10th century), Bhaṭṭa Tauta (10th century), Mammaṭa Bhaṭṭa (11th century), Mahima Bhaṭṭa (11th century), Abhinavagupta (11th century), Tilaka (11th century), Ruyyaka (11th century) and so on. Even though Kashmir's tradition of literary science began with Bhāmaha's *Kāvyālaṅkāra* in the 7th century, what gave it a real impetus was the reign of King Jayāpīḍa in the 8th century. King Jayāpīḍa was the grandson of King Lalitāditya, the celebrated patron of art and science. Lalitāditya's reign was followed by an age of political turmoil and a consequent lull in intellectual and creative exercise. Jayāpīḍa who wished to restore his grandfather's era of glory generously funded both the intellectuals and creative writers in Kashmir. According to Ingalls, 'It was under King Jayāpīḍa that school of literary criticism in Kashmir originated' (1990: 5). Kalhaṇa's *Rājataraṅgiṇī* talks highly about Jayāpīḍa's reign. According to *Rājataraṅgiṇī*, 'By him [Jayāpīḍa], learning which had hidden itself far away, was made to appear [again] in this land which was its original home just as the Vitastā by Kaśyapa' (I; 165). As far as *kāvyaśāstra* is concerned, this crucial movement was led by two major intellectuals namely Udbhaṭa and Vāmana.

Udbhaṭa and Vāmana's texts systematised Sanskrit poetics in terms of its size, style, and approach. First of all, the critical corpus of Vāmana and Udbhaṭa alone is as large as all the earlier works on poetics put together. Udbhaṭa was the first literary critic to borrow verses from an independent literary work to explicate various critical concepts. While Udbhaṭa's predecessors like Bhāmaha and Daṇḍin created independent verses to demonstrate figures of speech and literary tropes, Udbhaṭa borrowed explanatory verses from his own creative work *Kumārasambhava* which deals with the birth of Kumāra, the son of Śiva and Pārvatī. Vāmana, Udbhaṭa's successor, even incorporated poems from other creative writers of his period. Through his *Kāvyālaṅkāra-sāra-saṃgraha*, Udbhaṭa also set a new model for the composition of treatises on literary science by approaching a core text with a succession of commentaries (Bronner 2016: 85).

After Jayāpīḍa's reign, the second crucial landmark in the history of *kāvyaśāstra* in Kashmir occurred during the rule of King Avantivarman of the Utpala dynasty in the 9th century.[9] It was in Avantivarman's court that the great literary theorist Ānandavardhana produced his famous *Dhvanyāloka* which revolutionised Sanskrit literary science through the concept of *dhvani*.[10] After the death of King Avantivarman (883 CE), courtly patronage for literature and literary criticism again had a setback.

During the reign of Śankaravarman in the late 9th century and that of Queen Didda in the mid-10th century, Sanskrit literary production once again got arrested in Kashmir because of political turmoil. Didda's reign was particularly a period of rebellion and violence.[11] The withdrawal of royal patronage during the time of Śankaravarman and Didda resulted in a near dearth of literary production in Kashmir. We have no Sanskrit lyric or play from Kashmir during this period. The only *mahākāvya* that is available from this period is Abhinandana's *Kādambarī-kathā-sāra*. However, the tradition of Sanskrit scholarship, especially that of Śaiva philosophy and *kāvyaśāstra*, continued to flourish chiefly because of the Brahmans living in the capital or on their tax-free grants of land. They made sure that their sons were trained in grammar and other scholarly disciplines in Sanskrit (Ingalls 1990: 28–29). So, we have a lot of texts on literary theory from both the 10th and 11th centuries such as Bhaṭṭa Nāyaka's *Hṛdayadarpaṇa*, Dhanañjaya's *Daśarūpaka*, Bhaṭṭa Tauta's *Kāvyakautuka*, Kuntaka's *Vakroktijīvita*, Abhinavagupta's *Abhinavabhāratī*, Mahima Bhaṭṭa's *Vyaktiviveka* and Mammaṭa's *Kāvyaprakāśa*.

In the 12th century, under King Harṣa's reign, Sanskrit learning in Kashmir again faced a serious crisis from which it could never survive. The last major *kāvyaśāstra* text to be circulated outside of Kashmir was *Alaṅkāraratnākara* of Śobhākaramitra from the end of the 12th century (Pollock 2001: 396). The 12th century is considered the endpoint of the early phase of *kāvyaśāstra* on two grounds. First of all, it marks the end of Kashmir's prominence as the centre of Sanskrit learning in general and *kāvyaśāstra* tradition in particular. Second, the post-12th century phase is characterised by the emergence of the vernacular literary tradition and the dwindling of Sanskrit's monopoly as the language of science and literature. The corpus of writings that Sanskrit *kāvyaśāstra* tradition produced during the entire span of the early phase, starting from the 7th century to the 12th century, can broadly be classified into eight schools such as *alaṅkāra, rīti, guṇa, doṣa, dhvani, vakrokti, anumāna* and *aucitya*.

The Medieval Phase or the Age of *Navya*s

From around the 13th century onwards, the second phase in the history of Sanskrit *kāvyaśāstra*, which I call 'the medieval phase', begins. The criticism that was conventionally directed against Sanskrit poetics in the medieval phase was that there was nothing worth mentioning in Sanskrit literary theory during the medieval period. For scholars like S.K. De, the Medieval phase was a period of mere imitation and restatement of old critical idioms.

However, scholars like Bronner show us that Sanskrit poetics in the medieval phase was equally innovative and powerful. It is important to note that despite the strong influence of vernacular literature, during this phase, Sanskrit *kāvyaśāstra* continued to produce new treatises, thereby ensuring the continuum of its great lineage dating back to the 7th century. Some of the major *kāvyaśāstra* texts that were composed in this phase include Singabhūpāla's *Rasārṇavasudhākara* (14th century); Bhānudatta's *Alaṅkāratilaka*, *Rasamañjarī* and *Rasataraṅgiṇī* (16th century); Rūpa Gosvāmi's *Nāṭakacandrikā*, *Ujvalanīlamaṇi* (16th century); Prabhākara Bhaṭṭa's *Rasapradīpa* (16th century); Keśavamiśra's *Alaṅkāraśekhara* (16th century); Appayya Dīkṣita's *Vṛttivārttikā*, *Kuvalayānanda* and *Citramīmāṃsā* (16th century); Jagannātha's *Rasagaṅgādhara* (17th century) and Viśveśvara

Pandita's *Alaṅkārakaustubha, Rasacandrikā, Kavīndrakaṇṭhābharaṇa, Alaṅkārapradīpa* and *Alaṅkāramuktāvali* (17th century).

Bronner's observation on this matter is worth mentioning here:

> A remarkable trend of innovation seems to characterize Sanskrit Poetics on the eve of colonialism. Like intellectuals in other Sanskritic disciplines, *ālaṃkārikā*s—from about mid-sixteenth-century onward—adopted a new discursive idiom, composed in novel genres, demonstrated a fresh interest in the history of their tradition, and worked across disciplines at a hitherto unknown rate. Moreover, they often had a clear sense of themselves as breaking new ground and were thus conceived by their colleagues. (2002: 441)

Bronner says that the medieval phase of Sanskrit poetics is particularly characterised by two events—one, a methodological change in the approach of Sanskrit *kāvyaśāstra*, and the other, the emergence of vernacular literature and poetics.

According to Bronner, the literary theoreticians in the medieval phase attempted to constitute a new relationship with their past. Instead of inventing any radically new critical concepts like *dhvani* or *vakrokti*, they directed their energy mainly towards critically examining the views of their predecessors and answering old questions in new ways (Bronner 2002: 456). To mark their departure from their predecessors in terms of their mode of operation and views, these new literary theoreticians identified themselves as *navya* or 'new', in contrast to their antecedents who they called *prācīna*s or ancients. A case in point is Appayya Dīkṣita's *Citramīmāṃsā* that meticulously attacks the claims of literary theoreticians from the previous period. In *Citramīmāṃsa*, Appayya Dīkṣita innovatively redefines the figure of speech called *upamā* or simile. Appayya sees simile as the archetypal *alaṅkāra* that functions as the base of all figures of speech. He envisions simile 'as the one and only actress on the stage of *kāvya*' (Bronner 2002: 444). Although Appayya is not the first critic to grant such a status to simile, the way he conceives simile is something distinct from his predecessors. Acknowledging the potency of the simile to generate other *alaṅkāras*, Appayya compares it to the concept of Brahman in the phenomenal world. Just as Brahman takes on various shapes, so also *upamā* in the figurative realm assumes the shape of different figures of speech. The way he presents *upamā* in *Citramīmāṃsā* is also in conjunction with his Vedantic disposition of the same. Appayya Dīkṣita even broke many existing conventions regarding the format in which a treatise in literary theory should be composed. Until Appayya's intervention, there had been an unwritten rule in literary science that while presenting a figure of speech, a critic should necessarily define that figure of speech. Appayya departed from this age-old practice by not defining what *upamā* is. This was to send a message that just as the essence of Brahman defies all ontological specificities, so also *upamā* refuses to be reduced to one particular definition. In his introduction, Appayya states that his definitions and illustrations are mostly drawn from the works of the ancients (*prācīna*) such as Mammaṭa, Vidyānātha, Bhoja and Ruyyaka. But as soon as his discussion begins, we learn that his invocation of the views of the ancients is not to blindly follow them but to challenge and modify them (2002: 445).

Jagannātha's *Rasagaṅgādhara*, another treatise on Sanskrit poetics from the medieval period, further criticises Appayya. In *Rasagaṅgādhara*, Jagannātha takes Appayya to task for introducing in *Kuvalayānanda* a new subspecies of the figure of speech called *apahnuti* (denial). According to Jagannātha, the proposed subtype cannot be considered a subcategory of 'denial' as it is not mentioned in the definitions of the category given in the previous treatises like Mammaṭa's *Kāvyaprakāśa*, Ruyyaka's *Alaṅkārasarvasva* and Appayya's own *Citramīmāṃsā* (Pollock 2001:16). Jagannātha's *Rasagaṅgādhara* was also noted for his disagreements with many of his predecessors. One such instance of critical dissent in *Rasagaṅgādhara* revolves around the question of whether *bhakti* should be considered a tenth *rasa*. Rejecting the position of his Vaishnavite predecessors like Rūpa Gosvāmi, Kavi Karṇapura and many others, Jagannātha says that *bhakti* cannot be considered a *rasa*, as it is against the dictum of writers like Bharata (2001: 15). Jagannātha's debate on the causes of *rasābhāṣa* or the semblance of *rasa* in *kāvya* is also noteworthy in this context. According to the *prācīna*s or ancients, a woman having multiple male partners is not a case of *rasābhāṣa*, if she is married to them. But for *navya*s like Jagannātha, this is a clear case of *rasābhāṣa*. Therefore, he says that Draupadī's love for her five husbands, unlike what his predecessors think, is a clear case of *rasābhāṣa*. Distancing himself from the old school and calling himself *navya* or new, Jagannātha declares: 'Here Draupadī's love for her husbands is an instance of *rasābhāṣa* or semblance of *rasa*. This is the view of the new intelligentsia. But the ancient scholars do not see a heroine's love for her multiple partners as a case of *rasābhāṣa*' (1888: 101). The instances I have cited here are just a small selection of cases in which medieval literary theorists established novel connections with their predecessors. Additional examples in this vein encompass Siddicandra's *Kāvyaprakāśa-khaṇḍana* and Jagannātha's *Citramīmāṃsā-khaṇḍana* which unmistakably challenge the assertions made in Mammaṭa's *Kāvyaprakāśa* and Appayya's *Citramīmāmsā*. These works clearly demonstrate that the medieval era of Sanskrit poetics was not merely a time of reiterating the old critical paradigms, but rather an active period of critical reflection and re-evaluation.

Another significant characteristic underpinning this phase is the great influence that Sanskrit *kāvyaśāstra* exercised upon vernacular poetics. Almost all *bhāṣa*s that produced treatises on literary science in the medieval phase drew considerable inspiration from Sanskrit *kāvyaśāstra*. G.N. Devy's observation is noteworthy in this context. According to Devy, the impact of Sanskrit poetics upon vernacular poetics was so strong that the vernacular languages failed to produce an indigenous tradition of *kāvyaśāstra* independent of their Sanskritic counterpart. Devy observes, 'The temporal sequence of events in the process of transition ought to have been: (i) decline of Sanskrit as a literary language, (ii) emergence of the *bhāṣa*s, (iii) decline of Sanskrit poetics and emergence of *bhāṣa* criticism' (2009: 66). But this logical sequence of events was defied when *bhāṣa* literature did not produce a literary theory on its own. The two most important deviations from this logical sequence that Devy notes are '(a) Sanskrit poetics does not show signs of decline several centuries after the emergence of *bhāṣas* criticism, and (b) no significant criticism in the *bhāṣas* traditions is in evidence' (2009: 66).

Even the treatises on poetics written in vernacular languages were either translations or pale copies of well-known works in Sanskrit poetics. For example, *Līlātilakam*, the *lakṣaṇagrantha* (the treatise that sets down rules) of Maṇipravāḷam—the medieval literary language—was very much modelled on the tradition of Sanskrit poetics. Like Sanskrit poetics which aimed to create a trans-local language for *kāvya*, *Līlātilakam* also generated a trans-regional literary language by mixing Sanskrit and *Keralabhāṣa*. *Līlātilakam* defines the literary language of Maṇipravāḷam as '*bhāṣā samskṛta yogo maṇipravāḷam*' (a blending of Sanskrit and *Keralabhāṣa*') (1969: 21). This tendency of standardising a specific language for literary production is something that *Līlātilakam* directly derives from Sanskrit poetics. According to Bhāmaha, the author of *Kāvyālaṅkāra*, Sanskrit, Prākrit and Apabhraṁśa are the only three languages fit for literary production (1998: 6).[12] In every aspect of *kāvya* that *Līlātilakam* deals with, there is evidently a stamp of Sanskrit literary theory. Rich Freeman observes, 'It [*Līlātilakam*] applies all of the technical apparatus of Sanskrit literary treatise that processes mundane language into poetry (*kāvya*)' (2003: 448).[13] About the influence of Sanskrit literary science upon the production of *kāvya* in classical Kannada, D.R. Nagaraj observes: 'Sanskrit was not only the language of the gods, it also behaved like a god itself. By the time the *Kavirājamārga* appeared on the scene, the attempt to create a vernacular double of Sanskrit was at its peak . . .' (2003: 335).[14]

The same was the case with Brajbhāṣa which borrowed considerably from Sanskrit poetics to form its vernacular counterpart. Busch says, 'For all their [Brajbhāṣa writers'] apparent radicalism in eschewing the time-honoured language of courtly intellectual life, and the trumpeting of their vernacular works as new theorizations, many early Brajbhāṣa scholars insist that they have not departed from existing Sanskrit tradition' (2004: 49). According to Busch, one of the primary sources of inspiration for Keśavdās's (16th century) *Kavipriya*, his manual for poets in Brajbhāṣa, is undoubtedly Daṇḍin's *Kāvyādarśa* (49). His *Rasikpriya*, yet another work of literary science, is modelled on Rudra Bhaṭṭa's *Śṛiṅgāratilaka*. Busch opines,

> At first glance the *Rasikpriya* appears to be a very close adaptation of the *Śṛṅgāratilaka* (Ornament of Passion) by the Sanskrit rhetorician Rudra Bhaṭṭa (ninth-century?). Keśavdās follows virtually the same order of treatment of the subject matter as his source, and significant lexical borrowings in the definition verses show his reliance on Rudra Bhaṭṭa to be beyond doubt. (50–51)

Cintāmaṇi Tripathi (17th century), one of the major intellectuals to emerge after Keśavdās, in his *Kavikulkalptaru* openly proclaims his indebtedness to Sanskrit poetics for serving as a model for his own treatise on poetics in Brajbhāṣa: 'I, Cintāmaṇi, have carefully considered the precepts of books written in the language of the gods [i.e., Sanskrit], and I am expounding a theory of vernacular literature' (quoted in Busch 2004: 50).[15] Similar is the observation of Bhikaridas (18th century), another great rhetorician in Brajbhāṣa. He says, 'I studied the Sanskrit texts/*Candrāloka* and *Kāvyaprakāśa* /I understood them,/And made their ideas beautiful in the vernacular' (quoted in Busch, 52). These examples corroborate the argument that the literary theorists of vernacular poetics always looked up to Sanskrit poetics as a model. This does not imply that the vernacular traditions of poetics did not introduce anything new on their own. On the other hand, the point I want to emphasise here is that Sanskrit literary science was indeed a great source of influence and inspiration for the treatises of literary science in vernacular languages.

'Reconstructionist and Disseminationist' Phase

The beginning of the third phase in the history of Sanskrit *kāvyaśāstra* which I would like to name the 'reconstructionist and disseminationist' phase coincides with the start of the colonial period in India. It is interesting to note that even during the colonial period, scholars continued to produce treatises in Sanskrit poetics. A few cases in point in this respect include Cirañjīva Bhaṭṭācārya's *Kāvyavilāsa* (18th century), Hariprasāda Māthura's *Kāvyārthaguṃpha* (18th century), Garaḷapurī Śastrı's *Kṛṣṇabhūpalīyam* (19th century), Caṇdamārutācārya's *Citramīmāmsodhara* (19th century), Rama Pisharody's *Dhvanyalokalocanākhyāyikā*, *Kuvalayānandavyākhyāyikā* and *Citramīmāmsāvyākhyāyikā* (19th century), Acyutācārya's *Sāhityasāra* (19th century) and Gulāba Rāva Mahārāja's *Kāvyasūtrasaṃhita* (19th century).[16]

Although the scholarship (*pāṇḍitya*) in Sanskrit scholarly tradition continued to flourish during this period, 'the capacity of Sanskrit thought to make history had vanished' (Pollock 2000: 1) by the time this phase ended. Pollock observes that 'the production of moral-legal texts, for example, which was so extensive throughout the 17th-century, ceased entirely [during this time], and in core disciplines like hermeneutics or literary theory no significant scholarship—that is, significant in the eyes of the tradition itself—was again to be written' (2000: 1). Though none of the treatises in Sanskrit poetics from this period made history, this phase in the history of Sanskrit poetics is marked by two seminal activities: (i) the reconstruction of many *kāvyaśāstra* texts that were thought to be lost forever and (ii) the translation of many *kāvyaśāstra* texts from Sanskrit to English and other vernacular languages.

A representative case in point in this regard is the reconstruction of Kuntaka's *Vakroktijīvita*. Kuntaka's *Vakroktijīvita* which was long thought to be lost and known only through the citations in the later texts of *kāvyaśāstra* is now available to us primarily through the efforts of S.K. De and K. Krishnamoorthy. S.K. De brought out a copy of Kuntaka's *Vakroktijīvita* in 1923 based on two Devanagari transcripts of a Malayalam manuscript (which was also lost at some point) from the Oriental Manuscripts Library, Chennai. The manuscript seemed to have contained four chapters, but the last chapter in the manuscript broke off without any conclusion. The third chapter also contained a lot of gaps in it. So De was unable to publish a readable text. However, he brought out an edition of Kuntaka's *Vakroktijīvita* with the first two chapters and a resume of the contents of the last two chapters (De 1961: iv–x). This arrangement was still necessary even in the second edition in 1928 when a new edition of *Vakroktijīvita* was brought out after a new manuscript was found in Jaisalmer. Despite these limitations, his edition was quite crucial in introducing Kuntaka's idea of *vakrokti* to the readers of modern India. A coherent and readable text of *Vakroktijīvita*, along with a translation, came out in 1977 through the efforts of Krishnamoorthy. For this edition, Krishnamoorthy collected a transcript of the last two chapters of the Madras manuscript and combined it with the same portions of the new Jaisalmer manuscript and the *Vakroktijīvita* extracts in the *Kalpalataviveka*. For the first two chapters, he made use of the Jaisalmer manuscript along with De's 1928 edition. These efforts finally came to fruition in the form of a readable text for *Vakroktijīvita* (Lariviere 1980: 323). Almost all other key texts of Sanskrit poetics that we now have access to have gone through similar processes of editing and careful textual scrutiny during this period.

The second term in the title of the third phase, that is, 'dissemination' has two senses to convey—the dissemination of the texts of Sanskrit literary theory through printing and the dissemination of the knowledge about Sanskrit literary theory through the translation of these texts into English and other vernacular languages. The vital force behind this process was obviously the publishers of the classical series such as the Bibliotheca Indica, Gaekwad Oriental Series, Nirnayasagar Press, Motilal Banarsidass, Anandashram Sanskrit Series, Trivandrum Sanskrit Series and so on. It should be noted that the concern of these publishers was not particularly the publication of *kāvyaśāstra* texts but Sanskrit classics in general. They published a lot of rare Sanskrit books which were available only in manuscript form till then. The translations of many key texts of Sanskrit *kāvyaśāstra* into English and other languages also played a vital role in disseminating knowledge about Sanskrit poetics among modern scholars who could not read and understand the original texts written in Sanskrit. Some of the most prominent works in this direction include S.K. De's translation of Kuntaka's *Vakroktijīvita*; Manomohan Ghosh's English translation of Bharata's *Nāṭyaśāstra*; Vavila Venkateswara Sastralu's translation of Daṇḍin's *Kāvyādarśa*; George Hass's translation of Dhanañjaya's *Daśarūpaka*; C. Sankara Sastri's translation of Daṇḍin's *Kāvyādarśa*; Krishnamoorthy's English translation of Abhinavagupta's *Abhinavabhāratī*; Vāmana's *Kāvyālaṅkārasūtravrtti*; Mammaṭa's *Kāvyaprakāśa* and Kṣemendra's *Aucityavicāracarcā* and *Kavikanṭhābharaṇa*.

The Pragmatist Phase

The fourth phase of Sanskrit *kāvyaśāstra* is the pragmatist phase. This phase which began in the mid-20th century and became particularly prominent in the last quarter of the same century was characterised by an inquiry into the pragmatic use of Sanskrit literary theories in the field of contemporary literary criticism in India. We saw that in the olden days, literature was considered a special form of language which could be crafted only after careful and dedicated practice in *kāvyaśāstra*. Many Sanskrit literary theoreticians had emphasised the role that proper training in poetics played in the production of literary texts. Daṇḍin's observation about the importance of education in *kāvyaśāstra* is a representative case in this regard. According to Daṇḍin, 'Just as a blind person cannot distinguish between different colours, so also a poet untrained in poetics cannot differentiate between poetic merits and faults' (1962: I.8.16). He went on to say that a poet, irrespective of whether he is naturally endowed with poetic genius or not, can master the art of poetry simply by learning and practising *kāvyaśāstra* (I.104). According to Bhāmaha, an aspiring poet should venture into composing *kāvya*s only after achieving mastery over all the *śāstra*s related to *kāvya* (1998: I.10.18). Vāmana held that a poet should understand the *guṇa*s and *doṣa*s of *kāvya* by getting educated in *kāvyaśāstra* (2000). Even if a person is naturally endowed with poetic talent, s/he should definitely undergo training in poetics (*Kāvyālaṅkārasūtravrtti*, I.1.4.5). In his *Kāvyamīmāṃsā* (10th century), Rājaśekhara emphasised the importance of education in *kāvyaśāstra* by saying that '[t]he prior knowledge of *śāstra* is essential for the appreciation of *kāvya*'. According to him, 'Just as nothing is visible in the dark without the aid of light, so also no poet can create [poems] without the knowledge of *śāstra*' (20.20). All these observations attest to the fact that mastery over *kāvyaśāstra* was as important as *pratibhā* (inborn genius) to become a *kavi*. Familiarity with the technicalities underpinning a literary artefact was also necessary for the readers/critics of Sanskrit *kāvya* to appreciate literary works. This conception remained unchanged even when vernacular literature took shape during the medieval period. The very existence of texts in vernacular poetics—for instance, *Līlātilakam* in Malayalam, *Kavirājamārga* in Kannada or *Kavikulkalptaru* in Brajbhāṣa—attests to this fact.

But, by the mid-20th century, a new conception of literariness (which already began in the 19th century under the influence of Western literature) started taking deep root in the Indian subcontinent. This new approach tried to replicate the style and cadence of everyday speech in literary works and consequently stood in contrast to the Formalistic notions about literature to which Sanskrit *kāvyaśāstra* conformed. In other words, the erstwhile conception that one needs to know about the lessons of Sanskrit poetics before attempting to compose a literary work altogether disappeared. By this time, the literary world in India was also making a transition from Sanskrit to English and the vernacular languages which mostly embraced and championed this new conception of literature through new genres like the novel, short story, autobiography, etc. What engendered a radical break from this conventional notion of literariness was obviously the educational policies of the colonial government. An important aspect of colonial education was the introduction of Western literature in schools and universities. The new genres of literature from the West such as the novel, short story, essay, etc., which stood closer to the style of workday language, played a vital role in replacing the old conception of literariness with a new one.

Under the influence of this new literary sensibility, there arose a strong feeling among many vernacular critics that the parameters of Sanskrit criticism were not adequate to judge and appreciate the new literary works founded on a new sense of literariness. K.C. Anthappayi's *Bhāṣānāṭakapariśodhana* is a case in point. In *Bhāṣānāṭakapariśodhana*, Anthappayi vehemently criticised the predilection of Malayalam playwrights for Sanskrit dramas. He argued that critics should abandon the practice of *guṇanirūpaṇam*—which involved analysing Malayalam dramas based on the traditional literary merits endorsed by Sanskrit poetics—since the literary sensibility of both the readers and writers had radically changed under the influence of the new genres. We would soon see this suspicion about the relevance of Sanskrit poetics first echoed by scholars such as Anthappay, slowly growing in magnitude.[17] For example, K.M. George highlights the inefficacy of Sanskrit poetics in modern times in connection with Malayalam literature:

> In the olden days, literature was essentially in verse and in India the language was Sanskrit. In order to enable the average sahṛdaya to enjoy literature, there was a need for commentaries and interpretations. It was therefore natural that external apparatus like rhyme, rhythm and figures of speech was expounded by scholars: this was an accepted aspect of criticism, construed by some as the be-all and end-all of criticism. When works came in nālikera pāka (like a coconut), the hard shell had to be broken and the kernel shown. So this kind of criticism developed in Malayalam and it was quite relevant when classics appeared in the maṇipravāla style. Even in the modern period when we deal with the poems of Kumaran Asan and Vallathol, though the shell is not hard, a similar analytical approach had some relevance. But criticism had to take a fresh turn, to explore and explain the spirit of the work, which was more elusive than the external aspects. And when fiction came to the force, a completely different approach was called for. The form itself was Western and works were mostly in draksha paka (like grapes) and hence the analysis of the external structure had no relevance. What was necessary was to unravel the spirit of the work and to arouse the reader's dormant sensibility to full participation. Who wants a commentary for Thakazhi's Chemmeen, written in the colloquial language? (1973: 86)

Like George, many literary critics in Malayalam sought the employment of a new set of parameters for the appreciation and analysis of modern literary works which shared the style and sensibilities of everyday speech and life. Satchidanandan in his 'Dilemmas of Indian Literary Criticism' further observes,

> The new textures of urban living with its contradictory aspects of penury and luxury, the intensification of the alienation among the intelligentsia; the angst of the new awareness of space and time; the growing consumer instinct; the loss of traditional values and the growth of the new post-industrial ethos made possible by new technologies, etc. proved that 'traditional critical frameworks are hopelessly inadequate to meet the needs of literary criticism which declared their independence from Sanskrit centuries ago, even while retaining aspects of it that they found useful to their flowering and growth'. (2014)

According to him, 'this crisis which is often unacknowledged had already begun with the maturing of Indian languages.' It is also important to note that this phase is marked by the sheer absence of any new treatises in literary theory in Sanskrit, let alone any new critical concept. One would be surprised to note that well-known scholars of Sanskrit *kāvyaśāstra* in the 20th century such as S.K. De, P.V. Kane, C.D. Narasimhaiah, M. Hiriyanna, Krishna Chaitanya, K. Krishnamoorthy, Raghavan and so on did not produce a single new treatise in Sanskrit poetics, although they were very much involved in building the intellectual history of this epistemology.

At this juncture, it is also important to mention the nativist approach or *desivad* propounded by scholars like G.N. Devy. Devy, in his 'After Amnesia: Tradition and Change in Indian Literary Criticism' (1992), holds that neither Sanskrit poetics nor Western criticism is sufficient to interpret the literary works in the *bhāṣa*s of the Indian subcontinent since the concerns of literature in the *bhāṣa*s are considerably different from those of Sanskrit poetics and Western criticism. Considering 'criticism as a cultural subsystem rather than a web of abstract theoretical constructs' (2), Devy opines that 'literature growing out of one type of underlying linguistic and metaphysical structure cannot be understood and studied by criticism growing out of another and alien type of underlying linguistic and metaphysical structure' (143). He says,

> Sanskrit literary and critical traditions are accessible to the modern intellectual only as imaginary possessions. The modern Indian critic *can* say that India had glorious tradition of literary criticism a thousand years ago. But, having said this, he is unable to use this tradition as a living tradition which shares a frame of reference within which his normal intellectual activity takes place. (30)

The same criticism, says Devy, holds water in the case of Western criticism also. The fundamental problem that Devy has with Western criticism is that the application of theoretical positions born out of the cultural milieu of Europe fails to yield any result in our studies of native texts (16). Therefore, he insists that each *bhāṣa* should develop a native mode of criticism of its own, instead of banking upon Sanskrit and Western criticism. Devy talks about what he reckons to be the predicament of *bhāṣa* literature in modern times and suggests a possible solution:

> All these writers and critics sharing a common present can nonchalantly refer to so many different traditions and past ages. Rarely does one find instances of systematic efforts at understanding contemporary literature on the basis of knowledge embedded in native literary traditions. Among these exceptions one can count are Bhālchandra Nemade and his associates in the nativist school of criticism.[18] (15)

In spite of this feeling that Sanskrit poetics is outdated to appreciate modern literary works, a small group of critics during the 1980s attempted to apply Sanskrit *kāvyaśāstra* to evaluate the merit of modern literary works from India. This shift which can be labelled as a 'revivalist trend' was spearheaded by Indian literary theoreticians such as K. Krishnamoorthy, Krishna Rayan, Ayyappa Paniker, C.D. Narasimhayya and others. The seminal event which inaugurated this movement was a seminar held at the Literary Criterion Centre at *Dhvanyāloka* in Mysore, on the theme of 'the Formulation of a Common Poetics for Indian Literature Today'. The seminar paid considerable attention to the practical use of Sanskrit poetics as a common critical framework to effectively understand and judge the literary merit of Indian literary texts in modern times. The conference concluded that the *rasa-dhvani* approach, being the most dominant critical system in the Indian literary context, could be used as a common critical framework to evaluate literary texts of Indian origin.

The book *The Burning Bush* (1988), edited by Krishna Rayan, was an immediate output of this thought. This book analyses 17 literary works from 17 different Indian languages through the lens of the *rasa-dhvani* approach in order to understand the practical applicability of these theoretical positions in modern criticism. The blurb of the book says,

> With literature in the various Indian languages interacting more vigorously today than ever before, it has become all-important that critical practice in them shares a common theoretical framework, so that the assumptions, analytical tools, and evaluative criteria used are roughly uniform. Obviously, there are major advantages in evolving this framework from existing Indian theory rather than sources elsewhere. The most widely dominant Indian critical system is the Rasa-dhvani theory formulated in the 9th century. But before adopting it, it must be revised in the light of other Indian and Western theories, and it must also be tested on texts in Indian Languages. It is this latter that Krishna Rayan's book [The Burning Bush] seeks to do.

Krishna Rayan's *Rasa-Dhvani and Present-day Literary Theory and Criticism*; Ayyappa Paniker's *The Renovation of Rasa-theory*; Krishnamoorthy's *The Relevance of Rasa Theory to Modern Literature*; R.B. Patankar's *Does the Rasa Theory Have Modern Relevance?*; Umashankar Joshi's *The Relevance of Sanskrit Poetics to Contemporary Practical Criticism*'; etc., are some of the major works in this direction

This strong urge to go back to the literary concepts in classical languages, in fact, originated from a desire to develop an alternative model of literary criticism and to decolonise Indian critical sensibility from Western literary concepts. This praxis, they thought, would 'reconstitute a sense of Indianness of the texts considered, and assess their virtue by the standards and assumptions of indigenous aesthetics' (Ashcroft and Tiffin 2002: 173). Ashcroft and Tiffin talk about this tendency in literary criticism in *Empire Writes Back*:

> Indian scholars and critics have been locked in debate as to how far these traditions can be adapted to the needs of modern criticism for Indian literature. The debate centres on whether or not the 'highly sophisticated theories' propounded by the Sanskrit 'schoolmen' can be, or, indeed, ever were 'applied in the evaluation of works of art' (Krishnamoorthy 1984) and, more specifically, whether the terms

> of this tradition: *rasa, dhvani, alaṅkāra*, etc., are more relevant and suitable than imported terms to the description of contemporary literatures in the Indian vernacular languages and, to a lesser extent, to Indian literatures in English. (116)

My study is also positioned in the pragmatic phase of Sanskrit literary science, in the sense that it aims to answer the question whether Sanskrit literary theories, which played a vital role in setting literary standards for almost a millennium, have any scope and relevance in the contemporary literary scene. Nonetheless, I do not intend to follow the path that the pragmatist phase is currently following. That is to say, I do not subscribe to the view that Sanskrit literary theories can be used to judge the literary merit of a work of literature in modern times. This does not mean that I subscribe to the view that Sanskrit *kāvyaśāstra* is an exhausted field of research, and in contemporary criticism, its scope is that of a museum piece. My approach to Sanskrit *kāvyaśāstra*, on the other hand, emphasises the production of new knowledge about and from these theoretical positions through constant re-readings of *kāvyaśāstra* from multiple perspectives. The next chapter of the book which is titled 'Beyond the Canon' elucidates my approach to Sanskrit *kāvyaśāstra* and explains the reasons why I disagree with the current trends in the pragmatist phase.

1

Beyond the Canon

Sanskrit literary theories in their canonical form always constituted an attempt to identify the formal devices that create 'literariness' in a work of literature. The chief motive behind this praxis was the assumption that knowledge about the factors that generate 'literariness' in *kāvya* would contribute greatly to the production of good art. In response to this enquiry into the soul of literature, Sanskrit literary theoreticians came up with different formal elements such as *alaṅkāra*, *rīti*, *guṇa*, *dhvani*, *vakrokti*, *aucitya*, etc., as the building blocks of literariness. In spite of their differences of opinion regarding the prioritisation of these formal elements in terms of their contribution to 'literariness', they all had a consensus on the idea that 'literariness' is largely a textual entity.

We know that the idea of literariness changes over time. Today 'literariness' is a functional category. In other words, it is the reader who constructs 'literariness' as opposed to certain special textual elements creating 'literariness' in a work of literature. In this scenario, do Sanskrit literary theories that attempt to understand the ontology of 'literariness' have any relevance? This chapter takes its cue from this dilemma that the practitioners of Sanskrit literary theories encounter in the present age and tries to problematise the scope of Sanskrit literary theories in the contemporary scene of research. This chapter is divided into three sections. The first section is an examination of how Sanskrit *kāvyaśāstra* conventionally approached literature. The second section exposes the inefficacy of practising Sanskrit *kāvyaśāstra* in the way it was originally conceived and practised in the early period, and finally, the third section proposes the necessity of a new course of action in the field of Sanskrit *kāvyaśāstra* theories.

Kāvyaśāstra and the Ontological Approach

Sanskrit *kāvyaśāstra* always held an ontological view of literature. That is to say, it believed that it is the presence of certain special linguistic features, such as poetic suggestion, figures of speech, figurative deviation, etc., that attribute literariness to a work of art. Therefore, throughout its history of almost a millennium, Sanskrit *kāvyaśāstra* was exclusively preoccupied with the task of identifying and analysing the formal devices generating literariness in a work of art. Considering *kāvya* as a 'special and specialised' mode of language, marked by the 'ingenious' use of certain distinctive linguistic devices, *kāvyaśāstra* always made it a point to delimit *kāvya* from the other uses of language, such as *śāstra*, the *Veda*s and workaday language.[1] We have a host of literary theoreticians in Sanskrit poetics who typify this exclusionist view of literature. For example, Bhāmaha, who is considered the founding father of literary theory in Sanskrit, distinguishes *kāvya* from workaday language and music. He says that a literary work should always be marked by *vakrokti* or the deviant utterance, and expressions that are matter-of-fact and bereft of *vakrokti* will continue to remain *vārtā* or report (1998: II.87). Similarly, a composition which is smooth, clear and elegant but devoid of *vakrokti* will become only music, not *kāvya* (I.34). Similar opinion is aired by Abhinavagupta who in his commentary on Ānandavardhana's *Dhvanyāloka* separates the remit of *kāvya* from that of the *Veda* and workaday language. Abhinavagupta says, 'Both everyday sentences and Vedic sentences have meaning without being poems' (1990: 75). Hemacandra in *Kāvyānuśāsana* says that it is the presence of four components, namely *śabda* (signifier), *artha* (signification), *guṇa* (poetic qualities) and *alaṅkāra* (figures of speech), that constitutes a *kāvya* (33). Vāgbhaṭa II delimits the ambit of *kāvya* by defining it as a composition of *śabda* (signifier) and *artha* (signification) marked by the absence of *doṣa*s and the presence of *guṇa*s and *alaṅkāra*s (14). Mammaṭa observes that 'It [*kāvya*] consists in word and sense—without faults and with merits and excellences of style—which may at times be without figures of speech' (1966: 4).[2]

In *Candrāloka*, Jayadeva also sets the limit of poetic expression by defining *kāvya* as a verbal icon characterised by the absence of *doṣa*s and the presence of *lakṣaṇā* (deviant utterance), *rīti* (diction or style; literally means 'path'), *guṇa*, *alaṅkāra*, *rasa* (aesthetic emotion) and *vṛtti* (linguistic modality) (I.7). Vidyānātha in *Pratāparudrīya* saw *kāvya* as a special composition of both *gadya* (prose) and *padya* (poetry), bereft of *doṣa*s and adorned by *guṇa*, *alaṅkāra*, *śabda* and *artha* (II.1). Bhaṭṭa Nāyaka talks about three crucial components that were conspicuously absent in other uses of language and present only in *kāvya*. According to him, these three elements are *abhidhāyakatva* (denotative function), *bhāvakatva* (ability to evoke aesthetic experience) and *bhogakṛttva* (the experience of aesthetic emotion). In his commentary on *Dhvanyāloka*, Abhinavagupta later reproduces this view of Bhaṭṭa Nāyaka (1990: 2.4 L). Kuntaka opines that the figurative deviation of speech (*vakrokti*) makes *kāvya* different from ordinary expression and the use of language in *śāstra*s (1977: 291). According to Bhoja, although poetry is called the combination of word and meaning, not all compositions of word and meaning could claim the status of a *kāvya*. In *Śṛṅgāraprakāśa*, Bhoja makes a clear distinction between *kāvya* and other linguistic genres based on the nature of the language employed in them. According to Bhoja, workaday language is the explicit language of science and daily life. *Kāvya*, on the other hand, is the deviant language found in texts teeming with aesthetic pleasure (I.221).[3] We can see this view of *kāvya* as a special linguistic category with complex literary conventions and elaborate metrical schemes, unchangingly going down the line, till the end of the active phase in Sanskrit literary culture in the 17th century, with Jagannātha observing that *kāvya* is a special combination of word and meaning, with beautiful words denoting noble significations (*ramaṇīyārthapradipādakaḥ śabdaḥ kāvyaṃ*) (1888: 4).

According to Gerow, 'the problem of *kāvyaśāstra* was then seen in differentiating that particular expression we call poetic from other verbal means, *śāstra,* and narrative' (1977: 224), and throughout its history of almost a millennium, *kāvyaśāstra* 'never ever strayed away from this central problem' (219). In other words, *kāvyaśāstra* was incessantly preoccupied with the task of pinpointing factors that were responsible for the specificity of poetic language. Pollock observes,

> What substantively constitutes *kāvya* and how literariness comes into being were naturally matters of on-going debate, and various elements were proposed as the essence of *kāvya*. But the fact that *kāvya* has an essence—a 'self' or 'soul', as it was phrased—something marking it as different from every other language use was never doubted by anyone. (3)

This identification and scrutiny of formal factors that made *kāvya* a 'special' use of language was primarily motivated by the hope that a proper understanding of the textual elements responsible for the unique nature of *kāvya* would contribute greatly to the creation of good art (Pollock 2003: 44; Sivarudrappa and Rao 1985: 78).

In their endeavour to identify the 'soul' or the most important formal constituent of *kāvya*, different literary theoreticians privileged different formal elements as the inalienable mark of literature. Samudrabandha, a 10th-century commentator on Ruyyaka's *Alaṅkārasarvasva*, gives us a glimpse into this. In his commentary on *Alaṅkārasarvasva*, Samudrabandha observes,

> Literature is marked by certain special words and meaning. The speciality of these two [i.e. *śabda* and *artha*] can be analysed in three ways—through some language feature [*dharma*] or through some function [*vyāpāra*] or through aesthetic suggestion [*dhvani*]. The first group contains two sects—the one that gives importance to figures of speech and the one that lays emphasis on poetic qualities. In the second sect, some pay attention to beautiful expression and

> the others to the capacity to produce aesthetic pleasure [in readers]. Of these five groups, the first one is accepted by Udbhaṭa and others; the second one is accepted by Vāmana, the third one by the author of *Vakroktijīvita*, the fourth by Bhaṭṭa Nāyaka and the fifth by Ānandavardhana.[4] (1915: 14)

Although there were differences of opinion among literary theoreticians as to which of these elements has to be treated as the most important element of *kāvya*, they all had a consensus on the idea that *kāvya* is a unique use of language. Therefore, their efforts were unidirectionally oriented towards unravelling the various formal factors that attribute an aura of uniqueness to literature.

The term *alaṅkāraśāstra* which was often used synonymously with Sanskrit poetics readily functions as a pointer to the teleology of Sanskrit *kāvyaśāstra*. Because of *kāvyaśāstra*'s unwavering interest in the ornaments (*alaṅkāra*) of *kāvya* that made literature a higher-order linguistic composition, the term *alaṅkāraśāstra* was often used synonymously with *kāvyaśāstra*.[5] A survey of the major theoretical positions in Sanskrit literary theories such as *alaṅkāra*, *rīti*, *guṇa*, *vakrokti*, *dhvani* and *aucitya* will further corroborate this observation.

For Bhāmaha, the earliest known exponent of *kāvyaśāstra*, it is primarily *alaṅkāra*s or figures of speech that transform a piece of writing into *kāvya*. Therefore, in his *Kāvyālaṅkāra*, Bhāmaha is chiefly concerned with the identification and analysis of *alaṅkāra*s that beautify a work of literature. Bhāmaha, in his attempt to identify the unique nature of *kāvyaśarīra* or the body of *kāvya*, lists and analyses 38 *alaṅkāra*s. According to Bhāmaha, what makes an *alaṅkāra* different from other uses of language is its figurative deviation (*vakratā*) from ordinary language. Therefore, he employs the term *alaṅkāra* to refer to all the deviant linguistic expressions (1998: I.36).[6] Bhāmaha opines that a poet should always be diligent in developing this art of figurative deviation which functions as the characteristic mark of all *alaṅkāra*s. He notes, 'This peculiar method of statement (*vakrokti*) is found everywhere (i.e., in other *alaṅkāras*). By these meanings are rendered beautiful. Poets should be assiduous in cultivating it. Where is an *alaṅkāra* without this?' (II.85).[7] What Bhāmaha's theory of *alaṅkāra* shows is that *kāvya* is distinct from other uses of language by the presence of *alaṅkāra*s or figures of speech. So, his analysis of *kāvyaśarīra* is mainly oriented towards the identification and scrutiny of *alaṅkāra*s which present everything in a defamiliarised form.[8]

Daṇḍin, in his *Kāvyādarśa*, declares that the aim of his work is to identify the elements that make up the body of *kāvya*: 'Here [in *Kāvyādarśa*] I state the characteristic marks of *kāvya* [*kāvyalakṣaṇa*], after my careful study and scrutiny of the previous treatises' (I.2). In *Kāvyādarśa*, Daṇḍin broadens the scope of his scrutiny of *kāvyaśarīra* by increasing the number of figures of speech to 35 and that of poetic merits to 10. Considering the amount of attention he pays to the analysis of *alaṅkāra* and *guṇa*, we can safely assume that in Daṇḍin's conception, *kāvyaśarīra* is primarily constituted by *guṇa*s and *alaṅkāra*s.

Vāmana's *Kāvyālaṅkārasūtravrtti* opens with a chapter titled *kāvya-śārīra-nirṇaya* or the 'understanding of the anatomy of *kāvya*'. Such a self-explanatory title immediately informs us that the purpose of his work is to identify and analyse the formal factors that go into the making of the body of *kāvya*. Vāmana sees a *guṇa* or poetic merit as the vital force of literature. According to him, a verbal expression without *guṇa* cannot become a *kāvya*, just as a group of words without syntax cannot make a coherent meaning (2000: III.2.2–3).[9] He is of the view that a literary style (*rīti*) where all the *guṇa*s are properly knit together serves as the soul of *kāvya* (*rītirātmā kāvyasya* I.6).[10]

Ānandavardhana, the successor of Vāmana, criticises Vāmana's view that *rīti* is the soul of *kāvya*. According to Ānanda, 'It was persons unable to analyse the true nature of poetry . . . who propounded the doctrine of "styles"' (1990: 669). For Ānanda, *dhvani* or poetic suggestion is the soul of *kāvya* (*kāvyasayātmadhvanirīti*) (47). Therefore, in his *Dhvanyāloka*, Ānandavardhana examines the nature of *dhvani* in detail. Kuntaka, a 10th-century literary critic from Kashmir, considers *vakrokti* (figurative deviation of speech) as the chief source of literariness. According to Kuntaka, '*Kāvya* is that combination of *śabda* (signifier) and *artha* (signified) which shines forth with *vakratā* (figurative deviation of speech) to impart pleasure to readers' (1977: I.7). Considering *vakrokti* as the supreme governing principle of *kāvya*, Kuntaka makes a thorough analysis of the various forms of *vakrokti* in the four chapters of his *Vakroktijīvita*.

Kṣemendra, an 11th-century literary critic from Kashmir, holds that *aucitya* or propriety is the sine qua non of *kāvyaśarīra*. Unlike the literary theoreticians we have seen before, Kṣemendra does not introduce any new formal feature as the source of literariness. On the other hand, he lays emphasis on the proper organisation of the linguistic devices which are already considered by his predecessors as the hallmark of literature. He is of the view that in *kāvya*, the proper organisation of these distinct linguistic devices is as important as their presence. According to him, neither figures of speech nor poetic merits will look charming without propriety (1954: 118). Kṣemendra's concept of *aucitya* is an all-encompassing precept that is applied to all aspects of *kāvya*. Emphasising the importance of propriety in *kāvya*, Kṣemendra says 'Figures of speech are but ornaments, while merits of speech are mere excellences; but propriety is the abiding life of poetry, full of flavour' (118). 'Kṣemendra compares a poem that does not conform to the rules of propriety to an unruly person wearing his girdle string around his neck, necklace around the waist, anklets on the hands and bracelets on the feet' (119).

From this analysis, we can arrive at two major points that are central to this study—(1) the entire epistemology of *kāvyaśāstra* had a consensus on the idea that *kāvya* is a 'special' way of using language and (2) the chief concern of *kāvyaśāstra* was the identification and scrutiny of different linguistic elements responsible for the unique nature of *kāvya*.

The Juncture of Conflict

By the mid-20th century, a new conception of literariness (which already began in the 19th century under the influence of Western literature) also started taking deep root in the Indian subcontinent. This new approach tried to replicate the style and cadence of everyday speech in literary works and consequently stood in contrast to the Formalistic notions about literature to which Sanskrit *kāvyaśāstra* conformed. In other words, the erstwhile conception that one needs to know the lessons of Sanskrit poetics before attempting to compose a literary work altogether disappeared. By this time, the literary world in India was also making a transition from Sanskrit to English and the vernacular languages which mostly embraced and championed this new conception of literature through genres like the novel, short story, autobiography, etc.

It is also significant to note that there was a strong feeling among many vernacular critics that the parameters of Sanskrit criticism were not adequate to judge and appreciate the new literary works founded on a new sense of literariness. In connection with Malayalam literature, K.M. George observes,

> In the olden days, literature was essentially in verse and in India the language was Sanskrit. In order to enable the average sahṛdaya to enjoy literature, there was a need for commentaries and interpretations. It was therefore natural that external apparatus like rhyme, rhythm and figures of speech was expounded by scholars: this was an accepted aspect of criticism, construed by some as the be-all and end-all of criticism. When works came in nālikera pāka (like a coconut), the hard shell had to be broken and the kernel shown. So this kind of criticism developed in Malayalam and it was quite relevant when classics appeared in the maṇipravāla style. Even in the modern period, when we deal with the poems of Kumaran Asan and Vallathol, though the shell is not hard, a similar analytical approach had some relevance. But criticism had to take a fresh turn, to explore and explain the

> spirit of the work, which was more elusive than the external aspects. And when fiction came to the force, a completely different approach was called for. The form itself was Western and works were mostly in draksha paka (like grapes) and hence the analysis of the external structure had no relevance. What was necessary was to unravel the spirit of the work and to arouse the reader's dormant sensibility to full participation. Who wants a commentary for Thakazhi's Chemmeen, written in the colloquial language? (1973: 86)

What engendered a radical break off from this conventional notion of literariness during the colonial period was obviously the educational policies of the Empire. An important aspect of colonial education was the introduction of Western literature in schools and universities. The new genres of literature from the West such as the novel, short story, essay, etc., which resembled the style of workaday language, played a vital role in replacing the old conception of literariness with a new one.

The erstwhile ontological notion of literature on which Sanskrit *kāvyaśāstra* was founded could never again recapture the terrain of literature. Today literature is no longer an ontological category, as it used to be in the past. It has now completely become a functional category. In other words, according to the modern parameters of literariness, any piece of writing (be it a news item in a daily or a hoarding on the wayside or a railway catalogue) can become a literary work, provided the reader reads it poetically. This marked a paradigmatic shift from the ontological view of literariness to a functional, reader-oriented view of 'literariness'. Eagleton succinctly summarises this point in the following words:

> There is no 'essence' of literature whatsoever. Any bit of writing may be read non-pragmatically, if that is what reading a text as literature means, just as any writing may be read 'poetically.' If I pore over a railway timetable not to discover a train connection but to stimulate in myself general reflections on the speed and complexity of modern existence, then I might be said to be reading it as literature. John M. Ellis has argued that the term literature operates like the word 'weed':

> weeds are not particular type of plants, but just any kind of plant which for some reason or another a gardener does not want around. Perhaps 'literature' means something like the opposite: any kind of writing which for some reason or other somebody values highly. As the philosophers might say 'literature' and weed are functional, rather than ontological terms: they tell us about what we do, not about the fixed being of things. (1996: 10)

Like Eagleton, Stanley Fish also holds the same pragmatic view on literature. For Fish, 'It is not that the presence of poetic qualities compels a certain kind of attention, but that the paying of a certain kind of attention results in the emergence of poetic qualities' (1980: 326).[11]

These observations show that in the contemporary critical scene, the concept of literariness is primarily a functional and subjective category. This is squarely against the view of the exponents of Sanskrit *kāvyaśāstra* who treat literature purely as an ontological category. Pollock juxtaposes these two contradictory positions:

> What would be problematic, however, at least from the vantage point of contemporary theory, is claiming to know and define 'literary.' There are good reasons for rguing—and many have argued this for the past two decades or more—that anything can become literature; that the term needs to be understood pragmatically rather than ontologically, as pointing to ways certain texts are used rather than defining what those texts inherently and essentially are. Yet from the vantage point of premodern South Asia, most certainly not everything could be *kāvya*. (2006: 2)

Since 'literature' and 'literariness' are presently treated as functional categories, as opposed to the pre-given ontological categories, any attempt to define *kāvya* or identify the linguistic elements that attribute 'literariness' to a text will definitely become a futile endeavour. So, Sanskrit literary theories in their canonical form—that is, as an attempt to identify and analyse factors responsible for the unique nature of a literary work—fail to share a frame of reference in our contemporary critical scenario. The same holds for any attempt to use Sanskrit *kāvyaśāstra* as a mechanism to evaluate the literary merit of a work.[12] If a text does not contain any intrinsic 'literariness', how can we say that a particular critical framework is effective in judging a text's literariness or its authentic meaning? If this is the case, do Sanskrit literary theories have any contemporary relevance in the area of research?

In Search of Future Possibilities

We saw that Sanskrit poetics is canonically considered an attempt to understand and analyse the ontology of *kāvya* which was widely thought of as a special use of language, distinctly different from ordinary speech. To answer the question of whether Sanskrit poetics has any relevance in the contemporary literary scene, we need to ask another question: Is our canonical understanding of Sanskrit *kāvyaśāstra* (that is an attempt to understand the source of literariness) the only way in which this corpus of knowledge can be understood? In fact, we will have to answer this question in the negative because canonical reading is only one of the many ways in which a text can be read and understood, although we take for granted the canonical reading of a text as the most authentic and natural way of reading it. The major reason for considering canonical reading as the only or the most authentic way of reading a text is that canonical reading is a product of the cultural hegemony.[13] We know that a text never privileges any particular framework of reading as more authentic than others. It is the cultural hegemony prevalent in society that prefers certain kinds of reading to some other forms of reading. It persuades the readers to believe that canonical reading is the most authentic and natural way of reading a text. Paul de Man's observation in this regard merits attention here. He observes,

> There are no longer any standpoints that can a priori be considered privileged, no structure that functions validly as a model for other structures, no postulate of ontological hierarchy that can serve as an organizing principle from which particular structures derive in the manner in which a deity can be said to engender man and the world. All the structures are, in a sense, equally fallacious and are therefore called myths. (1996: 10)

Though no reading can a priori be considered more authentic than others, canonical reading often presents itself as the most authentic reading. It rules out all other readings as inauthentic and deviant, and functions as a restrictive force upon a text's potential to produce infinite meanings. In other words, it literally 'prunes' a text, thereby giving it a fixed signification and a permanent generic label.

So, it is important to understand that the treatises that constitute Sanskrit literary science are ultimately 'texts'. According to Barthes, 'the Text is plural' in the sense that it cannot be reduced to any permanent categorisation or any fixed order of signification. Barthes notes,

> The Text is plural. Which is not simply to say that it has several meanings, but that it accomplishes the very plural of meaning: an *irreducible* (and not merely an acceptable) plural. The Text is not a co-existence of meanings but a passage, an overcrossing; thus it answers not to an interpretation, even a liberal one, but to an explosion, a dissemination. The plural of the Text depends, that is, not on the ambiguity of its contents but on what might be called the *stereographic plurality* of its weave of signifiers . . . . (1986: 159)

Barthes distinguishes a Text from a Work. According to Barthes, while the idea of a Work imposes a permanent signification and a specific generic label on discourse, the Text opens up discourse to numerous possibilities of interpretation. At this juncture, we should also note that the ideas of a Work and a Text are not two separate entities. On the other hand, it is our attitudinal difference that makes a certain discourse a Work or a Text. If we attribute a definite meaning and a generic label to a discourse, then we consider it a Work, whereas if we hold that a discourse can have multiple meanings and generic labels, then we are treating it as a Text. It is to mark this radical attitudinal shift from the idea of monolithic signification to multiplicity of signification that Barthes employs the term Text. Therefore, in modern-day literary criticism, the conception of a discourse—be it a poem, a drama or a piece of literary criticism—is that it is a 'text' open to infinite possibilities of meaning. According to Barthes, 'To give a text an Author [a permanent signification] is to impose a limit on that text, to furnish it with a final signified to close the writing' (1986: 147). Barthes says that a Text is not a line of words releasing a single theological meaning' (146) furnished by the author. According to him,

> The fact is that writing can no longer designate an operation of recording, notation, representation, depiction, (as the classicist would say), rather it designates exactly what linguists, referring to Oxford philosophy, call a performative, a rare verbal form (exclusively given in the first person and in the present tense) in which the enunciation has no other content (contains no other proposition) than the act by which it is uttered. (145–146)

For Barthes, 'a text's unity'—that is, what it means in its entirety—lies in its 'destination' which is the reader. The point that Barthes wants to emphasise is that the meaning of a text is what the reader creates, as opposed to the author pre-determining it. Therefore, a critic's job is not to 'decipher' the authentic meaning of the text but to disentangle the infinite number of significations a text can generate in order to capacitate a text to perform 'what may be called an anti-theological activity'. Such an activity, Barthes says, 'is truly revolutionary, since to refuse to fix meaning is, in the end, to refuse God and his hypostases—reason, science, law' (148). Barthes not only shows us the essential nature of a text but also charts out a revolutionary plan of reading for critics.[14]

We saw that literature and 'literariness' being the constructs of the readers, any attempt to enquire into the factors that constitute literariness in a work does not have any relevance. In other words, the canonical way in which Sanskrit literary theories were practised fails to share a frame of reference today. Also invalid is our attempt to judge the literary merit of a work on the basis of the standards of literariness set by Sanskrit *kāvyaśāstra*. Does this imply that there is no room for further research in the field of Sanskrit literary theories beyond simply reiterating these concepts? This question has to be answered in the negative. In modern times, our research in Sanskrit literary theories should be oriented towards generating new knowledge about these theoretical positions by re-reading them from multiple vantage points, as opposed to endlessly re-enacting the same old canonical framework.

This existential question was not specific to Sanskrit studies alone. It was also invoked during the 1970s and 1980s with respect to English studies in the country. The whole discipline of English literature was introduced in the country to create a group of natives who are Indian in 'blood and colour', but English in tastes, opinions, morals and intellect. Sunder Rajan notes that the colonial project required both giving the ruling patriots a sense of possession of a great literature of their own and impressing the natives with the cultural superiority of the ruler. This dual purpose was achieved by introducing English literature into school and college curricula in both England and India. The crucial question looming large in front of the critics and teachers in the university was what to do with this discipline that carried the cultural baggage of the colonial past. Did we necessarily need a discipline that was once subtly used to subjugate the natives? Although this question could be somewhat satisfactorily answered by including works belonging to Indian English literature, the canon of English literature, which contained the so-called makers of English literature from Europe, continued to pose a problem. This conundrum was overcome with a radical change in pedagogy that enabled students to problematise texts in new ways, rather than using pre-existing frameworks to understand the Western world. Such a pedagogical praxis enabled students to challenge 'the implicit claims to universality' endorsed by these texts. A similar shift in pedagogical approach is essential in the realm of Sanskrit poetics, especially when it emphatically loses relevance in its traditional canonical structure.

Just as a poem, a drama or an article can be interpreted from multiple perspectives, so also the texts that constitute Sanskrit poetics can be revisited from a variety of vantage points. For this, we necessarily need to do away with our fetish for the rigid frameworks of canonical reading with which we have so far been dealing with these theories. In other words, we need to, as Derrida says, 'play' with these texts. The idea of 'play,' as Derrida conceives it, aims to explore a text's potential to produce an infinite number of significations without any teleological point of completion.

The Derridean Play and *Kāvyaśāstra*

Derrida in his essay 'Structure, Sign and Play: In the Discourse of Human Sciences' shows that conformity to a fixed centre stunts the production of knowledge, whereas 'play' which enables us to see an object from multiple perspectives helps us generate new knowledge. Any organisational mechanism which arranges a set of elements into a definite pattern can be called a 'centre'. Author, reader, god, idea, essence, etc., are a few examples of the idea of the centre. Without a centre, it is impossible to form a pattern. Acknowledging the importance of the centre, Derrida says that 'centre is necessary to orient; balance and organize the structure—one cannot in fact conceive of an unorganized structure' (1976: 352). But, he reminds us that our adherence to a fixed centre can also limit the 'play' or the infinite possibilities of interpretation. Derrida writes, 'Nevertheless, the centre also closes off the play it opens and makes possible. It is the point at which the substitution of contents, elements, or terms is no longer possible. At the centre, the permutation or the transformation of elements is always forbidden' (352). Derrida holds that any structure which is founded on a fixed centre is beyond the reach of 'play'. He says that so far we have been substituting one fixed centre with another, thereby negating the possibility of 'play'. The present time, Derrida opines, is marked by an 'event' which rejects the centre's position as a permanent locus. Now, the centre performs as 'a function, a sort of non-locus in which an infinite number of sign-situations come into play' (353), as opposed to functioning as an authoritative mechanism. For Derrida, any centre is only a provisional mechanism which inevitably and incessantly needs to be replaced by other centres through what he calls 'play'. 'Play' which poses resistance to any fixed referent keeps 'presence' or signification in a state of constant flux. Derrida says, 'Play is the disruption of presence . . . Play is always absence and presence, but if it is to be thought radically, play must be conceived of before the alternative of absence and presence' (369).

It is interesting to note that Derrida's idea of 'play', in many respects, draws parallels with Ādi Śaṅkara's concept of *līla*. Though functioning at a different level, the word *līla* in Sanskrit means 'play' or 'sport'. A key term in Advaita Vedānta philosophy, *līla* is the process by which the ultimate reality (whose true essence remains irreducible) called Brahman gets manifested in the world. Though Brahman is called the ultimate reality, its identity cannot be reduced to any fixed essence. In other words, the ontological status of Brahman defies all kinds of logical categorisations. Therefore, it is termed *nirguṇa*, that is, the one without any specific quality.[15] For Brahman, *māya* is the only *upādhi* or device by which It can make itself cognisable. Thus Brahman in conjunction with *māya* makes itself visible in infinite forms (1890: xxv). This process through which Brahman, in conjunction with *māya*, manifests itself in the world is called *līla*. *Līla* or 'play' is characterised by two features: It is performed without any purpose or teleological point of completion and there is no power that can control Brahman's play (*Vedāntasūtra* II.1.33). Comparing the process of inhalation and exhalation to Brahman's play or *līla*, Śaṅkara notes,

> We further see that the process of inhalation and exhalation is going on without reference to any extraneous purpose, merely following the law of its own nature. Analogously, the activity of the Lord also may be supposed to be a mere sport (*līla*), proceeding from his own nature, without reference to any purpose. (II.1.33)

Misra's observation on the concept of *līla* is also important here. He says,

> The fact is that Brahman can have no purpose in creating or manifesting the world. It cannot be guided or governed by any purpose in creating the world . . . And to say that Brahman has some purpose in creating the world will mean that it wants to attain through the process of creation something which it has not. And that is impossible. Hence there can be no purpose of Brahman creating the world. The world is a mere spontaneous creation of Brahman. It is a *līla* or sport of Brahman . . . The concept of *līla* signifies freedom as distinguished from necessity. (1998: 187)

There is no end to the play of Brahman. Nor is there any restriction upon *līla*. The entire elements in the world are different manifestations of Brahman brought about by Its play. There is also no distinction between Brahman and Its manifestations, as the term 'advaita' or non-dualism suggests. However, we cannot reduce the essence of Brahman to any of its manifestations. As is the case with the idea of *līla* in Advaita Vedantic philosophy, Derrida envisages 'play' as an infinite process which is resistant to all kinds of restrictions. Derrida's idea of 'play'. like the process of *līla* in Advaita philosophy, acknowledges all centres as true and real without treating any centre as the ultimate point.

This book is also a 'play' with the body of Sanskrit literary theories in order to explore the hitherto unexplored possibilities about this epistemology. We observed that there is no single way of reading a text, and it is the cultural hegemony that closes off other entry points to a text. Therefore the 'play' which I initiate in this study serves as a resistance to the policing forces that prescribe a permanent reading strategy for a text. Such a 'play' (which does not conform to any permanent plan or organisational pattern of reading), I hope, will be a liberating experience for these theories which were straitjacketed into the formulaic blocks of canonical reading. Each time we deconstruct or 'play' with a text, we create new knowledge about and from that text. Each new reading of a text dislodges the text from our taken-for-granted conceptions about it and leads us to the production of new knowledge about/from that text. An approach of this sort has given a new lease of life to many philosophical positions that were considered exhausted and outdated. A case in point is Nicholas Royle's re-interpretation of Freud in *The Uncanny*. In *The Uncanny*, Royle gives 'a series of close-readings of different aspects of the topic [the uncanny]' (2003: vii), thereby breaking free from the canonical reading prescribed for the understanding of the idea of uncanny.

In this context, I should also mention that 'play' is absolutely a reader-oriented mechanism in the sense that it saves the readers from being compelled to deal with a text in a rigid manner. By allowing the functioning of multiple centres, 'play' works against the totalising forces of fixed centres, such as canonical reading, which not only silences the infinite possibilities of signification in a text but also takes away a reader's opportunity to be 'creative' in the process of reading. In the execution of the canonical reading which follows a pre-determined plan of action, a reader is merely a consumer of the preconceived signification. Such reading gives the readers only a 'pleasure of consumption' and deprives them of the opportunity to rewrite or recreate a text. Barthes says,

> I can enjoy reading and rereading Proust, Flaubert, Balzac, and even—why not?—Alexandre Dumas; but this pleasure, however intense, and even when it is released from any prejudice, remains partly (unless there has been an exceptional critical effort) a pleasure of

> consumption: for, if I can read these authors, I also know that I cannot rewrite them. (1986: 63)

Thus, the canonical reading which prescribes a set of rules or criteria as to how to read a text restricts both the text and the reader. The idea of 'play' being the central methodological tool in my approach, this study can rightly be called a reader-oriented approach to Sanskrit literary theories. In the chapters that follow, I take these theoretical positions outside our canonical understanding so as to generate fresh perspectives about them and to shatter our veil of familiarity.

2

Avivakṣita-vācya-dhvani and the Restructuring of Conventional Semantic Ambit

In any language, the relation between signifier and signified is rigidly tied together by convention. By ascribing a set of specific meanings to each signifier, convention territorialises the semantic ambit of signifiers, thereby demarcating the range of significations each signifier can denote. The primary problem associated with this act of territorialisation is that it restricts a signifier's movement within a predetermined semantic field and consequently prevents it from representing new significations. In the act of mapping a definite semantic ambit for each signifier, convention also structures the individual users of language (which could be a speaker or listener or author or reader) by forcing them to confine themselves to a specific plan of dealing with the signifiers. Thus, the language user is rendered absolutely passive, as they have nothing new to contribute to the decoding of meaning, other than reproducing an already existing plan of functioning. It is precisely this structuring tendency of the convention that gets challenged in Ānandavardhana's *avivakṣita-vācya-dhvani*, which escapes the rigid semantic ambit that convention imposes upon a signifier through a process of deterritorialisation—a 'movement by which one leaves the [given] territory' (Deleuze and Felix 2005: 508). In this process, *avivakṣita-vācya-dhvani* offers a liberating experience, not only to the signifier but also to the individual users (both the author and the reader or speaker or listener) of the language who are otherwise forced by convention to accept the signifiers in a specific fashion.

From the canonical point of view, Ānandavardhana's theory of *dhvani* is an answer to the age-old question of what constitutes literariness in *kāvya*. Ānanda's major thesis statement in *Dhvanyāloka* is that the primary constituent of literariness or the soul of *kāvya* is *dhvani* (*kāvyasyātma dhvaniriti*; 1990: 47). Ānandavardhana wrote his famous *Dhvanyāloka*, dealing in extenso, with the ontology of *dhvani*, as reply to his detractors who argued that *dhvani* does not exist and is not the soul of *kāvya*. Ānandavardhana observes,

> Some have said that the soul of poetry, which has been handed down from the past by wise men as 'suggestion' (*dhvani)*, does not exist; others, that it is an associated meaning (*bhākta*); while some have said that its nature lies outside the scope of speech: of this [suggestion] we shall here state the true nature in order to delight the hearts of sensitive readers.[1] (47)

Ānanda, who places the suggestive poetry or *dhvani kāvya* on the highest pedestal, argues that *dhvani* is the life force of an ideal *kāvya*.[2] In the present study, I do not intend to reproduce, much less agree with, the canonical notion that a piece of writing necessarily needs to have *dhvani* to become a *kāvya*. On the contrary, in this chapter, I turn my attention to a new idea that remains yet un-theorised in the theoretical position of *dhvani*, that is, *avivakṣita-vācya* variety of *dhvani* is a resistance to the conventional semantic ambit imposed upon a signifier. By breaking off from the canonical order of interpretation, conventionally imposed upon the theory of *dhvani* and releasing the text to new possibilities of understanding, I also intend to liberate myself from the traditional and standard structure of approaching this theoretical framework. This study is also characterised by the reflections and interventions of two readers of *Dhvanyāloka* who are separated by almost a millennium, one Abhinavagupta (11th century), the commentator on *Dhvanyāloka*, and the other, me, a modern scholar of *dhvani* from the 21st century.

Convention and the Semantic Ambit

Before analysing how *avivakṣita-vācya-dhvani* transgresses the conventional semantic ambit of a signifier so as to release the signifier to a new signification that is not conventionally associated with it, it is important to problematise the very idea of convention. Convention is generally defined as 'the way in which something is done, that most people in a society expect and consider to be polite or the right way to do it'. Bourdieu calls this 'generally accepted "right" way to do something' *doxa*—a collective term for all the taken-for-granted truths in society. In his interview with Terry Eagleton, Bourdieu explains the idea of *doxa* by citing the example of a very common criterion by which students are often judged at school. At school, what serves as a measuring rod for a student's success is his/her performance in academics. If one does not score well in academic subjects, one is not considered good enough. Bourdieu says,

> I will give you an example taken from our society. When you ask a sample of individuals what are the main factors of achievement at school, the further you go down the social scale the more they believe in natural talent or gifts—the more they believe that those who are successful are naturally endowed with intellectual capacities. And the more they accept their own exclusion, the more they believe that they are stupid, the more they say, 'Yes I was no good at English, I was no good at French, I was no good at mathematics.' (2012: 268–269)

Even though scores in academic subjects do not take into account a lot of other factors that very much go into the making of a successful individual, people, for no apparent reason, tend to assess a child's excellence on the basis of his/her academic achievements. Common beliefs in society, such as this, constitute what Bourdieu calls *doxa*. Even without a rationale, *doxa* conveys a sense of being the correct approach to doing things. Within the ambit of *doxa*, says Bourdieu, 'the world of tradition [is] experienced as a "natural world" and taken for granted' (164). In other words, 'the established cosmological and political order is perceived in as . . . a self-evident and natural order which goes without saying and therefore unquestioned' (166). According to Bourdieu, 'Every established order tends to produce . . . the naturalization of its own arbitrariness' (164). The dominant classes in any society always 'have an interest in defending the integrity of *doxa*, or short of this, of establishing in its place the necessarily imperfect substitute, orthodoxy' (169). Now, is it possible to make a change in the existing *doxa*? A change in the existing convention or *doxa* can be made only by the dominant power structure in society, and an ordinary individual has no agency to alter it overnight. The primary problem with *doxa* is that it provides us with a specific set of dos and don'ts or a definite plan, and strongly disapproves of any deviation from it.

What we call *doxa* or convention pervades all walks of our lives, and even the language we speak is not outside of its clutches. Numerous conventions govern a language, encompassing aspects such as vocabulary, grammar, writing style and orthography, among others. These conventions lay out a series of rules for language users, expecting them to adhere to these rules when using the language. For example, the sentence constructions such as these—'he work very hard' or 'you speaks well'—are considered wrong in English because the convention or *doxa* governing English grammar insists that in simple present tense, we need to appropriately add '-s' or '-es' or '-ies' to the base form of the verb if the subject belongs to the category of third person singular. Similarly, according to the rules of English 'orthography', if I spell the word 'know' as 'no' or 'psychology' as 'sykology', I will be considered wrong in my use of language.

In the process of structuring a language, convention also structures the language users by way of prescribing them certain rules and regulations. Roland Barthes' observation in this regard merits attention here. Barthes says,

> Jakobson has shown us that a speech system is defined less by what it permits us to say than what it compels us to say. In French (I shall take

> obvious examples), I am obliged to posit myself first as subject before stating the action which will henceforth be no more than my attribute: what I do is merely the consequence and consecution of what I am. In the same way, I must always choose between masculine and feminine, for the neuter and the dual are forbidden to me. Further I must indicate my relation to the other person by resorting to either *tu* or *vous*; social or affective suspension is denied to me. Thus, by its very structure my language implies an inevitable relation of alienation. To speak, and, even with greater reason, to utter a discourse is not, as is too often repeated, to communicate. It is to subjugate: the whole language is a generalized reaction. (1977: 5)

According to Barthes, language which is structured by the rules of convention always controls its speakers. Because of this domineering nature of convention, Barthes says, the performance of the system of language is always fascist in nature: 'But language—the performance of a language system—is neither reactionary nor progressive; it is quite simply fascist; for fascism does not prevent speech, it compels speech' (5).

The same convention is also at work in the relation between a signifier and a signified. According to Saussure, a linguistic sign is a combination of two elements such as a 'concept' and a 'sound-image'. He calls the 'concept' part of a sign a 'signified' and 'the sound-image', a 'signifier.' Although a signifier 'has no natural connection with the signified' (1959: 69), the signifier, says Saussure, is 'not free, with respect to the community that uses it' (71). In other words, the signifier–signified dyad is always purely a heritage of the preceding period; a contract has been formed between concepts and sound-images. According to him, the only force that can bring about a change in the signifier–signified dyad is tradition: 'Because the sign is arbitrary, it follows no law other than that of tradition, and because it is based on tradition, it is arbitrary' (74). The crux of Saussure's argument is that although the signifier–signified dyad is arbitrary, it is rigidly bound by convention, and no individual user of language can arbitrarily make a change in the signifier–signified relation. Many Indian philosophers, especially the *Naiyyayika*s and *Vaiśeṣika*s, also have the same opinion. They hold that the relationship between a signifier and signified or *pada* and *padārtha* is a matter of pure convention.[3]

The conclusions that we can draw from these observations are these: (1) the relation between a signifier and signified is arbitrary; (2) although the signifier–signified dyad is arbitrary, they are rigidly bound together by convention, and normally, convention is the only force that can constitute a new relation between a signifier and a signified, and individual language users do not have the authority to influence this process; (3) convention demarcates a clearly defined territory or 'semantic ambit' for each signifier and prevents a particular signifier from transcending its semantic ambit to enter into the semantic ambit of another signifier; (4) not only does convention structure a signifier, it also coerces an individual user of a language (an author and a reader, a speaker or a listener) to limit his/her movements within the pre-set semantic ambit. In other words, within the conventional semantic ambit (the range of significations that a word is conventionally allowed to signify), the individual user of the language is deprived of creativity in the sense that s/he is merely following a plan that has already been set for them. To say the least, a signifier's mobility within a conventional semantic ambit is limited to a fixed territory, and the individual user of the language is normally denied an opportunity to exercise his/her agency in the deterritorialisation of the semantic ambit.

What Is *Avivakṣita-vācya-dhvani*?

Having examined how convention impacts signifiers as well as the individual users of language, in this section, we will see how Ānandavardhana's *avivakṣita-vācya-dhvani* poses resistance to the clearly defined conventional semantic ambit in order to give agency to the individual users of a language. But before that, it is necessary to have an overview of the idea of *dhvani* in general. The idea of *dhvani*, though in a different sense, was first used by the grammarians. Ānanda himself acknowledges this in his *Dhvanyāloka*:

> [T]he grammarians gave the name *dhvani* to the sounds of speech that are heard. In the same manner other wise men, who know the true essence of poetry have followed the example of the grammarians by giving the title *dhvani* to that verbal entity which contains a mixture of detonated elements and which is designated as 'a poem'. (1990: 1.13 I *A*)

Long before Ānanda wrote *Dhvanyāloka*, systematising the realm of *dhvani*, creative writers had already used the idea of poetic suggestion to its optimum in their works. It is evident from the various cases of *dhvani* that Ānanda cites from the works of his predecessors such as Vālmīki and Kālidāsa. Ānandavardhana's importance in the intellectual history of Sanskrit *kāvyaśāstra* rests primarily on the fact that he is the first critic to systematically theorise the concept of *dhvani*. Therefore, his *Dhvanyāloka* can rightly be called the *lakṣaṇa-grantha* (the rule-setting book) of *dhvani*.

According to Ānandavardhana, signification is of two types, namely literal (*vācya*) and suggestive (*pratīyamāna*). *Dhvani* is the ability of a signifier or a set of signifiers or a meaning—a sound or a gesture—to suggest something other than what it conventionally presents (1.1 e). These elements which function as a means to constitute suggestion are called a *vyañjaka* (suggestor) (III.1 *A*). Although Ānandavardhana opines that the idea of *vyañjaka* covers a wide range of linguistic and non-linguistic elements, his discussion of *vyañjaka* and *dhvani* in *Dhvanyāloka* is strictly limited to the linguistic realm. According to Ānandavardhana, *vyañjaka* within the linguistic field covers a wide variety of elements such as a *pada* (word), a *vākya* (sentence), a *varṇa* (phoneme), a *padāmśa* (a part of a word), a *saṃghaṭanā* (texture), an *alaṅkāra* (figure of speech), an *āṅgya* (gesture), a *sup* (case endings), a *tiri* (personal endings of a verb), *vacana* (grammatical number), *saṃbandha* (relationship indicated through the genitive), *kārakas* (complements of the verbal action, such as agent, object, locus, etc.), a *kṛt* (primary suffixes attached to the verb root), *sandhi* (compounds), etc. (3.15 *K*). During the process of suggestion, what a *vyañjaka* conventionally presents takes a back seat, and another thing that is not conventionally associated with it comes to the view of a *sahṛdaya* (a sensitive reader). According to Ānandavardhana, a *vyañjaka* implicates three things such as a *vastu* (a fact or a meaning), an *alaṅkāra* (a figure of speech) and a *rasa* (an aesthetic emotion). Ānanda says, '[T]he three areas within which suggestiveness operates are: the *rasa* and the like, certain types of *alaṅkāra* and facts or situations, provided they appear in suggested form' (3.33 i *A*).

Ānandavardhana divides the whole realm of *dhvani* into two broad categories such as *avivakṣita-vācya-dhvani* and *vivakṣitānya-paravācya-dhvani*.[4] Of these two varieties, what is of interest to me in this chapter is the first variety called *avivakṣita-vācya-dhvani*. According to Ānandavardhana, the term *avivakṣita-vācya* literally means that instance 'where the literal meaning is not intended' (II.1 *A*). In the case of *avivakṣita-vācya-dhvani*, what functions as a *vyañjaka* or 'suggestor' is a signifier. Ānanda divides *avivakṣita-vācya* into two varieties such as *atyanta-tiraskṛta-vācya* and *arthāntara-saṃkramita-vācya* (II.1 *A*). *Atyanta-tiraskṛta-vācya* is that type of *dhvani* where the literal sense of the signifier (*abhidhā*) is completely negated (3.33 j *A*). In *arthāntara-saṃkramita-vācya*, the literal meaning (*abhidhā*) retains certain elements of its primary sense but suggests a new meaning that is not conventionally attributed to it (3.33 j *A*). In *Vedāntasūtra*, Śaṅkara opines that if we completely negate the primary meaning of a term, it is impossible to generate a new meaning out of it (1890: IV I.6). Therefore, Ānanda's division of *avivakṣita-vācya-dhvani* into *atyanta-tiraskṛta-vācya* and *arthāntara-saṃkramita-vācya* is not on the basis of whether a word completely negates its primary meaning or not. On the contrary, it is based on the degree to which a signifier retains its primary meaning.

So, I must say that although Ānanda divides *avivakṣita vācya* into these two categories, namely *atyanta-tiraskṛta-vācya* and *arthāntara-saṃkramita-vācya*, it is impossible to categorically classify various instances of *avivakṣita-vācya* into *atyanta-tiraskṛta-vācya* and *arthāntara-saṃkramita-vācya*, since Ānanda himself does not propose any specific criteria to gauge the degree to which a signifier loses or retains its primary sense. Nevertheless, one thing we can say for certain is that in both these varieties, signifiers transcend their conventional semantic ambits and suggest a new meaning that is not conventionally associated with them.

The following is an example of the *atyanta-tiraskṛta-vācya* variety of *dhvani* (also known as *jahatsvārtha lakṣaṇā*) quoted by Ānanda in *Dhvanyāloka*:

> Though the sky is filled with drunken [*matta*] clouds
> and the woods with *arjunas* thrashing in the downpour
> these black nights too when the moon has lost its *pride* [*ahaṅkāra*]
> carry off my heart. (2.1 d *A*)

According to Ānandavardhana, this Prākrit verse, which describes a monsoon night, incorporates *dhvani* in the words 'drunken' (*matta)* and 'pride' (*ahaṅkāra*). The word 'drunken' (*matta*) means 'a state of inebriation due to the use of some intoxicant'. Since the condition of inebriation is applicable only to a sentient entity, the conventional meaning of the word 'drunken' (*matta*) is impossible in this context—we know that a cloud, being a non-sentient thing, cannot get intoxicated. So the word 'drunken' abandons its primary meaning and goes on to suggest one of the characteristics traditionally associated with a drunkard (as opposed to denoting the state of inebriation), which is 'the act of wandering around aimlessly'. Thus, the word 'drunken' undergoes an incorporeal transformation, that is, the physicality of the signifier does not change, but it takes on a new signification which is not conventionally associated with it. The same process happens in the case of the signifier 'pride' (*ahaṅkāra*). The word 'pride' literally means 'a feeling of pleasure or satisfaction that you get when you or people who are connected with you have done something well or own something that other people admire'. This is also a quality typical of a sentient creature, especially a human being. But this quality is attributed to the moon which is a non-sentient thing. Hence the literal meaning of the term 'pride' (*ahaṅkāra*) gets blocked and then the signifier deterritorialises its conventional semantic ambit to incorporate another meaning, that is, 'charm' (a positive quality which people can pride on). So, the sentence means that the moon has lost its charm.

Yet another example of *atyanta-tiraskṛta-vācya* that Ānandavardhana cites is from the *Rāmāyaṇa* of Vālmīki. This verse which describes Lakṣmaṇa's account of winter in Pañcavaṭī goes like this,

> The sun has stolen our affection for the moon,
> whose circle now is dull with frost
> And like a mirror *blinded* [*andha*] by breath
> shines no more. (1990: 2.1 c *A*)

Here *dhvani* resides in the word 'blind' (*andha*). The Sanskrit word *andha* means a person whose sight is destroyed. Here the word *andha* is superimposed on a non-sentient thing that is a mirror. In his *Locana* on this passage, Abhinavagupta notes that in the given context 'blindness cannot be applied even by an imaginary superimposition of this literal sense [for a mirror, being insentient, has no sight which could be destroyed]' (2 .1 c *A*). So, the primary meaning of the word is completely set aside to suggest a new meaning—'the incapability to shine' or 'the exceptional loss of beauty'. In this example, too, the physicality of the signifier remains the same, but its signification undergoes a transformation.

Now, let us look at the second variety of *dhvani* under *avivakṣita-vācya,* that is, *arthāntara-saṃkramita-vācya-dhvani. Arthāntara-saṃkramita-vācya* is that kind of *dhvani* where the literal meaning retains certain elements of its primary sense and then suggests a new meaning that is not conventionally attributed to it. A classic example of this variety of *dhvani* is *nagaraṃ praveśanti kuntāḥ* (the spears enter the city). In this example, the word 'spear' does not mean 'a weapon with a pointed tip'; rather, it means 'soldiers who wield the spears', that is, spearmen. Here, the word 'spear' retains its primary meaning to a greater degree because the persons here referred to are 'spearmen', not 'swordsmen' or 'bowmen'. So, the word *kuntāḥ* maintains certain aspects of its primary meaning, yet shows a new meaning that is not conventionally associated with it. The following is an example of *arthāntara-saṃkramita-vācya* that Ānandavardhana quotes in *Dhvanyāloka*:

> Virtues blossom
> When admired by men of taste
> When graced by the sun's rays
> a lotus becomes a *lotus* [*kamala*].

This verse which Ānandavardhana takes from his own *Viṣamabāṇalīla* refers to the point at which a *kāvya* attains perfection. The speaker says that just as a lotus reaches the pinnacle of its beauty when the sun showers its rays upon it, so also poetic qualities shine forth when they are appreciated by a connoisseur of art or *sahṛdaya*. In the given example, the suggestive word is 'lotus' (*kamala*) in its second occurrence. The word 'lotus' is conventionally used to refer to a tropical flower with white or pink petals which grows on the surface of lakes. In the aforementioned example, if we follow the conventional meaning of the word 'lotus', the line 'a lotus becomes a lotus' does not make any sense. Therefore, the term 'lotus' deterritorialises its conventional semantic ambit to suggest another meaning, that is, 'the actualization of all qualities that are supposed to be present in a lotus'. In other words, the word 'lotus' here means 'a state of perfection'. Thus, this line comes to mean that it is only when graced by the rays of the sun that a lotus reaches a state of perfection.

A glance at one more example will help us form a better idea of this variety of *dhvani*.

> Firmness, forbearance, self-control purity, pity, kindliness of speech, and constant faithfulness to friends: these are the seven *kindling-sticks* [*samidhāḥ*] to royalty. (372)

According to Ānandavardhana, in this verse, the word 'kindling sticks' (*samidhāḥ*) functions as a *vyañjaka* (suggestor). The word 'kindling sticks' (*samidhāḥ*) literally refers to the sticks used to kindle the sacrificial fire. In this context, the literal meaning of the word *samidhāḥ* gets blocked, since royalty is not a physical entity to be set on fire. Therefore, the word *samidhāḥ* comes to suggest a new meaning which is based on its function as a fuel—that is, 'to act as a medium to ignite something'. Here the signifier *samidhāḥ* or 'kindling sticks' loses its strong connection with fire and means 'a medium which can enhance the quality of something', in this particular context, royalty. So, according to Ānandavardhana, the word 'kindling-sticks' (*samidhāḥ*) in this verse serves as a *vyañjaka*, helping convey a figurative meaning where it symbolically represents a means to enhance or elevate the concept of royalty, rather than just its literal, physical use in kindling a fire.

Dhvani and Secondary Usage

In all these instances, the signifiers abandon their conventional denotative meaning (*abhidhā*) and present a new meaning that is not conventionally associated with it. According to Ānandavardhana, both these varieties of *avivakṣita-vācya-dhvani* perform deterritorialisation with the help of the secondary usage of signifiers (which includes various kinds of metaphorical and relational varieties) (3.33 i *A*). The concept of secondary usage can be summarised as the ability of a signifier to denote a new signification which is not conventionally associated with it, but somehow related to it. Śālikanātha in his *Vākyarthamatravṛtti* defines secondary usage as 'that which conveys a new meaning related to the sentence meaning through its primary sense, when that primary sense of the word is impossible in the sentence meaning' (13).

In Sanskrit, such words as *lakṣaṇā, upacāra, gauṇi* and *vṛtti* are interchangeably used to refer to the idea of secondary usage. Ānandavardhana uses two terms, such as *bhākta* and *guṇavṛtti*, to denote the secondary usage of words, and his term for the metaphorical variety of secondary usage is *upacāra*, and *lakṣaṇā* is the word that he reserves for the relational variety. Abhinavagupta, the commentator of Ānanda's *Dhvanyāloka*, employs the term *gauṇa* to signify the metaphorical variety and *lākṣaṇika* for the relational varieties. The sentence 'Devadatta is a lion' is an example of the metaphorical variety of secondary usage. In this example, the term 'lion' takes on a secondary sense because Devadatta, by no stretch of imagination, is a lion. Here, the conventional meaning of the term 'lion'—a large tawny-coloured cat living in prides—becomes impossible, and hence, it produces a new meaning that is culturally associated with the animal lion, say, for example, 'valour'.

The sentence 'I have read all of Shakespeare' is an example of one of the many varieties of relational variety. In this example, the term Shakespeare stands for the oeuvre of Shakespeare because of some relation other than the similarity between these two. If the metaphorical variety is based only on the common quality shared by the subject and the tenor, the relational variety can be of various types on the basis of 'conjunction', 'proximity', 'connection', 'opposition', 'relation of cause and effect', etc. This shows that there are numerous ways through which secondary usage can be employed to deterritorialise the conventional semantic ambit. Though Ānandavardhana does not mention the different methods employed by secondary usage to deterritorialise the semantic ambit of a signifier in *avivakṣita-vācya-dhvani*, it is worth exploring the observations of other theoreticians in this respect. Abhinavagupta, the commentator of Ānandavardhana's *Dhvanyāloka*, enumerates five major ways of making relational varieties. In his *Locana*, Abhinava says,

> And this relational variety is of five sorts, as it is based on (a) a conjunction [of the secondary object] with the direct object; for example, a direct object of the word '*dvirepha*' (possessing two r's) is the word '*bhramara*'—now the word '*bhramara*' is connected [by the conventions of language] with the six-legged creature, a bee; that object may be indicated by the word '*dvirepha*' because of the bee's connection with a direct object [of the word '*dvirepha*']; (b) the proximity (*sāmīpya*) of the secondary object to the direct object as in 'Village on the Ganges' [where the bank of the river is close to the direct object, river]; (c) *samavāya*, that is a connection: for example, 'Bring in the spears,' meaning bring the spearmen, [who are connected with the spears]; (d) opposition, as when one says with reference to an enemy, 'In what has he not benefitted from me'; (e) its being connected with the same activity, that is, when it is based on a relation of cause and effect: for example, 'he takes away my life,' when the expression is used of one who takes away one's food [here the direct object life is the effect of the secondary object, food]. In this way, *lakṣaṇā* occurs in all varieties. (1990: 1.18 *L*)

In all these five varieties of *lakṣaṇā*, a signifier abandons its popular meaning (*prasidhārtha*) and signifies a new meaning. Although Abhinavagupta mentions only five relational varieties, the possibilities of new varieties of *lakṣaṇā*s are definitely innumerable. Akṣapāda Gautama, in his *Nyāyasūtra,* mentions 10 ways of constituting secondary usages such as *sahacaraṇa* (association), *sthāna* (location), *tādarthya* (purpose), *vṛtta* (behaviour), *māna* (measure), *dhāraṇa* (weighing), *sāmīpya* (vicinity), *yoga* (conjunction), *sādhanā* (sustenance) and *ādhipatya* (supremacy) (1913: 60). In *Mahābhāṣya*,

Patañjali talks about four other ways to constitute secondary usage such as *tātsthyāt* (location), *tādharmyāt* (quality), *tatsāmipyāt* (proximity) and *tatsāhacaryād* (association) (1986: 218). As far as Jaimini is concerned, there are six bases for secondary usage such as *tatsidhi* (fulfilment of the intention), *jāti* (same origin), *sārūpya* (resemblance), *praśaṃsa* (eulogy), *bhūma* (predominance) and *liṅga-samavāya* (permanent connection with the indicative marker) (1923: 39–40). Nāgeśabhaṭṭa in his *Paramalaghumañjuṣa* adds *tādarthya* (intention) to the list of five mechanisms of secondary usage given by Patañjali (1986: 7). Mammaṭa (1966: II. 9–12), Viśvanātha (2016: II. 5–11) and Hemacandra (1964: 24–25) also suggest similar strategies to push a signifier to go beyond its literal meaning and suggest a new signification. This shows that there are innumerable possibilities to use secondary usages in a language.

Are All Secondary Usages *Dhvani*?

In the previous section, we saw that it is specifically the secondary usage with its numerous varieties that enables *avivakṣita-vācya-dhvani* transcend the conventional meaning. Now, a crucial question can emerge: 'Can all the secondary usages be elevated to the position of an *avivakṣita-vācya-dhvani*?' According to Ānanda, a secondary usage that has become part of the literary convention cannot become an *avivakṣita-vācya-dhvani*. According to Ānandavardhana, a secondary usage which has become part of convention or popular usage is only as good as the literal meaning. Therefore, he eliminates all instances of secondary usages that have become part of convention from the ambit of *dhvani*.[5] Ānanda opines,

> To this we reply that here also there is no fault; because while the type of suggestion where the expressed meaning is unintended [*avivakṣita-vācya-dhvani*] relies on the path of secondary usage, it is not itself secondary usage. Secondary usage can also be found [in instances that are entirely] without suggestiveness. (1990: 3.33 j *A*)

A secondary usage that has become part of the existing linguistic convention is called *nirūḍhā lakṣaṇā*, whereas the secondary usage where the speaker invents a new meaning, based on his/her intention (*tātparya*), is called *prayojanavatī-lakṣaṇā*. Kunjunni Raja observes that 'In the case of these faded metaphors [*nirūḍhā lakṣaṇā*] the association of the word with the original primary meaning has almost disappeared, and the word becomes an ordinary name for the actual referent without any other cognitive or emotive association' (2000: 263). In *Tantravārttika*, Kumārilabhaṭṭa holds that in *nirūḍhā lakṣaṇā*, the presence of secondary usage is forgotten to the point of treating it as the conventional primary sense of the signifier (643). What we call a dead metaphor in English—'a metaphor which has been so often used that it has become lifeless and lost its figurative strength' (Cuddon 1998: 186)—such as 'the leg of a table' is an example of *nirūḍhā lakṣaṇā*.

Ānandavardhana cites a lot of examples where *dhvani* does not occur even in the presence of secondary usage because that particular secondary usage is a *nirūḍhā lakṣaṇā*—a secondary usage that has become part of the existing linguistic convention. A case in point is the word *lāvaṇya*. Ānanda observes, 'Words such as *lāvaṇya*, which are used idiomatically in a sense other than their proper (etymological) sense, are never instances of *dhvani*' (1990: III.33 i *L*). The word *lāvaṇya* which literally means 'salty' is also used figuratively, by means of secondary usage, to mean 'charm' or 'beauty'. Even when the word *lāvaṇya* is used in the secondary sense to mean 'charm' or 'beauty', it cannot be considered an instance of *dhvani* because this secondary usage has lost its newness since it is already a part of the existing linguistic convention. Quoting Kumārilabhaṭṭa's *Tantravārttika*, Abhinavagupta says,

> As has been said, 'some cases of secondary usage, being idiomatic, so far as their force is concerned, are just like direct denotation.' Such words, although used in a sense different from their etymological sense, do not carry any *dhvani* and we cannot speak of *dhvani* in such cases. (1990: 1.16)

Abhinavagupta mentions many words such as *ānulomya, prātikūlya, sabrahmacārin,* etc., which, despite being cases of secondary usage, do not produce *dhvani*, as these secondary usages have become part of the existing linguistic convention (1.16 *L*).[6]

It is clear from this analysis that Ānandavardhana's *avivakṣita-vācya* variety of *dhvani* is a conscious attempt to break the conventional relationship between a signifier and its signification. What Ānandavardhana wants to practise is not the endless enactment of the same old frameworks of the signifier–signified relationship established by convention, but the creation of new structures which are hitherto non-existent. It should also be noted that the new meanings that *avivakṣita-vācya-dhvani* ascribes to a signifier are both provisional and conditional. Ānandavardhana says,

> A denotative power is the very self of each word, for the word is never known without it. But suggestiveness is not bound to the word, but *accidental,* for our apprehension of it is conditioned by context, etc. and it is not apprehended in the absence of those conditions. (1990: 577)

Such words as *matta* (drunken), *andha* (blind), *kamala* (lotus), *ahaṅkāra* (pride), *samidhāḥ* (kindling sticks), *kuntāḥ* (spears), etc., cannot have their new unconventional meaning outside certain specific contexts. This provisionality of the semantic ambit which is the very characteristic of *avivakṣita-vācya-dhvani* prevents a signifier from getting permanently territorialised and consequently becoming a part of the linguistic convention. Therefore we can conclude that *avivakṣita-vācya* perpetually aims to challenge the authoritarian disposition that convention takes towards a signifier–signified relationship.

The Creative Reader and *Avivakṣita-vācya-dhvani*

Avivakṣita-vācya-dhvani is a liberating experience not only for the signifier but also for the users of the language which include both the author/speaker and reader/listener. We know that within the rigid, conventional semantic ambit, the speaker of a language cannot transcend the pre-given territory. Nor can they 'create' any new order of signification for a word on their own. All they are allowed to do is choose an already-marked position within the existing territorial limit of the word. Therefore, during the actualisation of the conventional semantic ambit, both the author and the reader follow a pre-given structure. But *avivakṣita-vācya-dhvani* is a creative process which consistently demands the active participation of both the author and the reader. In *avivakṣita-vācya-dhvani*, the language user is consistently pushed to go beyond the already-existing conventional semantic ambit so as to ascribe a new sense to the signifier. This entrusts the language user with the task of 'breaking the veil of familiarity' about a signifier. To put it differently, the language user poses a strong resistance to what Harré calls linguistic essentialism which believes in the idea that a signifier has a fixed identity in the form of a set of fixed significations, and it cannot signify anything beyond its conventional significations (2002: 323).

We know that in the process of communication, the reader or listener holds an important position, as they are the ones who ultimately decode the meaning of an utterance. Therefore, it is very important to analyse the figure of the reader that *avivakṣita-vācya-dhvani* anticipates. In the *avivakṣita-vācya* variety of *dhvani*, the deterritorialisation of the conventional semantic ambit can be actualised only in the presence of a 'creative' reader who thinks beyond the possibilities of the conventional semantic ambit. No reader who confines himself/herself to the formulaic signifier–signified combination, set down by convention, can perform the deterritorialisation of semantic ambit. For a reader whose movement is controlled within the rigid conventional semantic ambit, *dhvani* fails to make any sense. This is because what functions as the soul or vital force of *avivakṣita-vācya-dhvani* is the hither-to untried combinations of secondary usage which demands that the reader or listener should experiment with the signifier. Kunjunni Raja talks about the process through which a reader broadens the semantic ambit of a signifier with the aid of secondary usage:

> Sometimes a word is used to denote a referent other than its normal one . . . If we take the word as denoting its normal primary meaning, the sentence may become nonsensical in the context. This produces psychic resistance in the listener, and there is a sort of break in the flow. It exercises attention and requires interpretation for understanding the purport. The actual referent of the word has to be taken different from its normal one, but in some way connected with it, either through similarity or through some other relation. (2000: 231)

So, the reader that *avivakṣita-vācya-dhvani* anticipates is not a conventional reader who confines himself to fixed semantic boundaries. An uncreative reader—a reader who sets out to create meaning only with his lexical knowledge—cannot deterritorialise the semantic ambit of a signifier in *avivakṣita-vācya* and actualise *dhvani*. The actualisation of conventional semantic ambit is primarily a matter of habit—'a more or less fixed way of thinking, willing, or feeling acquired through previous repetition of a mental experience' (Andrews 1903: 122). Here, the reader does not need to create anything new. In each context where the conventional semantic ambit is invoked, all that the reader or listener is supposed to do is choose one of the pre-given significations that suit the context. One's engagement with the conventional semantic ambit involves only the recollection of all the denotative meanings and the selection of one of those meanings that befits the context. Here, the reader or the listener is deprived of an opportunity to transcend the pre-given territory. But in *avivakṣita-vācya-dhvani*, no precognition about the meaning of the signifier is possible. Therefore the reader or the listener, in addition to their 'recollection' and 'selection' of the suitable primary meaning, will also have to deterritorialise the conventional semantic ambit to generate new meaning. Ānandavardhana notes, 'It [*dhvani*] is not understood by the mere knowledge of grammar and dictionaries. It is understood only by those who know the true nature of poetic meaning' (1990: 1.7 K). The true knowledge of poetic meaning here means the ability to move beyond the formulaic blocs of convention. In his commentary on this *kārika*, Ānanda continues,

> [T]his [suggested sense] is understood only by those who know the nature of poetic meaning. If this meaning were denotative, one would get to it by knowledge of literal, denotative meanings and the words that convey them. But this meaning is beyond the range of those who have taken pains only on the definitions of words and who have paid no attention to the poetic meaning, just as the character of the notes (*svara*s) and *śruti*s, etc. is beyond the range of those who know the definitions of music but are not good poets. (1.7 A)

This implies that, unlike the rigid semantic structures that convention imposes upon a signifier, *avivakṣita-vācya-dhvani* never keeps the territories of a signifier rigid for the reader. It invites from the reader a sort of 'play' or 'experimentation' with the signifier. By way of not offering an everlasting mechanism for decoding the signifier, *dhvani* constantly poses a challenge to the reader. Enhancing the reader's involvement in the production of meaning, *avivakṣita-vācya-dhvani*, Abhinava says, 'stands in need of something hidden, like buried treasure' (1990: 1.14 L). In the conventional semantic ambit of a signifier, both the author and the reader can afford to remain uncreative by blindly reproducing an already existing meaning. But in *avivakṣita-vācya-dhvani*, the reader and the author need to be equally 'creative' and active to respectively capacitate a signifier with poetic suggestion and deterritorialise the conventional semantic ambit.

In *Dhvanyāloka*, the term Ānandavardhana uses to refer to a reader or listener of *dhvani* is *sahṛdaya*. However, he does not specifically define the term *sahṛdaya* anywhere in *Dhvanyāloka*. Abhinavagupta's commentary on the term *sahṛdaya* in *Locana* says,

> The word *sahṛdaya* (lit., 'having their hearts *with* it') denotes persons who are capable of identifying with the subject matter, as the mirror of their hearts has been polished by the constant study and practice of poetry, and who respond to it sympathetically in their own hearts. (70)

The two key features that particularly characterise a *sahṛdaya* are these: They are capable of identifying with the subject matter and they respond to it sympathetically. This shows that the reader that *dhvani* anticipates is not a reader who sticks to a permanent and rigid structure. Rather, s/he is a sensitive reader who has the ability to sympathise with the subject matter in order to understand what the subject matter demands, as opposed to approaching it with a pre-determined plan of action. These two characteristics which define a *sahṛdaya* underlie the figure of the reader of *avivakṣita-vācya-dhvani* as well. We can say for certain that the reader that *avivakṣita-vācya-dhvani* anticipates is a *sahṛdaya* who sympathetically responds to a signifier in order to deterritorialise the rigid boundary of convention and create new meanings, instead of attributing a pre-given meaning to it. So, the primary prerequisite for a reader of *avivakṣita-vācya-dhvani* is that s/he should always be resistant to the act of reducing the meaning of a word to a set of pre-conceived significations. Only then can s/he sympathetically respond to *dhvani* and attribute a hitherto non-existent meaning to a signifier.

Privileging the position of the reader further, Ānandavardhana says that a reader's actualisation of *dhvani* need not always depend on whether the author or speaker intends *dhvani* in a particular context. According to Ānandavardhana, even if the author or speaker does not intend suggestive meaning in a particular context, a *sahṛdaya* has the freedom to come up with *dhvani*. Ānandavardhana says,

> A suggested sense which is revealed by word and meaning, if it is a specific intention, becomes a *vivakṣita* (something that the speaker wishes to convey), when it is revealed as the *tātparya* (final sentence meaning). However, this alone will not explain the term *dhvani*, which covers an immense area, because it is insufficient. Rather, it is a suggested element in any of the three forms, [*vastu*, *alaṅkāra* or *rasa*], *whether in the form of a speaker's intention or not*, if it is suggested as the final sentence meaning, that justifies the term *dhvani*, as we said in defining *dhvani* in terms of the aforesaid types of suggestiveness. (1990: III.33 m *A*)

The gist of what Ānanda says is that if a reader can 'create' the possibility of *dhvani* in a context—irrespective of whether the speaker/author intends it or not—that suggestive meaning, which *sahṛdaya* creates on his own, will fall in the ambit of *dhvani*. Daniel H.H. Ingalls explains the words of Ānanda:

> The *vyaṅgya* need not be intended by the speaker. A naive girl, to give an example not seldom used in Sanskrit poetry, may make a suggestion of which she is quite unaware and which she is so far from intending that she would avoid if she were. (1990: 583)

This can be better explained with the help of an example from Shakespeare's *King Lear* where the mentally deranged King Lear asks his companion Fool to unbutton his dress, upon feeling suffocated: 'Pray, undo my button' (Shakespeare 1918: 5.3.309). This request, being the words of an anguished father who sees the body of his beloved daughter, is, on the surface a banal request but suggests the depth of the misery that literally asphyxiates him. A creative reader can turn these words into an instance of *avivakṣita-vācya-dhvani* and say that what Lear actually wants the Fool to do is not just undo a few buttons, but save him from the ailments of his physical existence by undoing and removing the apparel of his life. It is of no consequence to speculate whether Shakespeare intended this range of meanings.

To summarise, we know that convention is a necessary evil in any language. It is called 'necessary' because language, being a cultural artefact, cannot function in the absence of convention. It is treated as an 'evil' because convention imposes a rigid structure upon language through rules and regulations embodied in the form of grammar, orthography, lexicon and so on. In our use of language, convention accepts only certain moves as valid, and anything outside the framework of convention is normally considered wrong and unacceptable. As far as the signifier–signified relationship is concerned, convention functions as a disciplinary mechanism, imposing a definite boundary upon a signifier. It is a disciplinary mechanism not only for the signifier but also for the speaker/author and listener/reader of the language who are forced to abide by the rules that convention prescribes. *Avivakṣita-vācya-dhvani* challenges this disciplinary mechanism that convention poses before the reader and the author by deterritorialising the conventional semantic ambit with the help of hitherto untried secondary usages. According to Ānandavardhana, *avivakṣita-vācya-dhvani* achieves deterritorialisation through the application of secondary signifiers, including various metaphoric and relational forms. However, secondary usages that have become ingrained within literary conventions, like 'the leg of a table' or 'the hands of a clock', cannot ascend to the level of *avivakṣita-vācya-dhvani*. This implies that *avivakṣita-vācya* is a conscious attempt to break the conventional relationship between a signifier and its signification. During the process of this resistance to the disciplinary mechanism of convention, *avivakṣita-vācya-dhvani* privileges three entities, namely, the reader, the author and the language by offering them a creative space to experiment with the already existing semantic ambit.

3

Aucitya: A Mechanism of Control

In early India, the reading of literature was primarily considered a spiritual activity aiming to liberate readers from their materialistic attachments. Aesthetic emotion or *rasa* was often considered a secular counterpart of spiritual bliss. Bhaṭṭanāyaka (10th century), as Abhinavagupta records it in his commentary on *Dhvanyāloka*, terms aesthetic experience as a special experience similar to the bliss of 'realizing [one's identity] with the highest Brahman' (*brahmasvadasahodara*; 1990: 222). According to Abhinava (11th century), '[t]he relishing of *rasa* is *alaukika* or supernormal' (191), and the process of aesthetic relish is *lokottararūpa* or 'something which transcends the experience of the workaday world' (1990: 195). Nevertheless, this did not mean that *kāvya* was absolutely removed from the constraints of the practical concerns of social life. In reality, *kāvya* was heavily controlled and tailored by the notions of *aucitya* or propriety prevalent in society. Scholars like Pollock, Raghavan, Kuppuswamy Sastri and so on had meticulously presented the social aesthetics of Sanskrit poetics and established the fact that *aucitya* always confined literary representations to the accepted social practices of the period.[1] In this chapter, I intend to put their observations in perspective to see how Sanskrit poetics in conjunction with the concept of *aucitya* (which is an aggregate of the moral and social ethos of the period) played a vital role in conditioning the readers, authors and the text of Sanskrit *kāvya*. Here, I argue that the social and aesthetic conditioning that *aucitya* performed in the realm of *kāvya* functioned at three interconnected levels: First, Sanskrit literary theoreticians conditioned the creative writers by instructing the rules of representation of character types and emotions through *kaviśikṣā*;

then the creative writers (who followed these rules of representation and literary composition) conditioned the creative artefacts as per the norms set by the theoreticians; and finally, the creative artefact shaped the moral and social ethos of the readers by functioning as a symbolic power. In all these three stages, *aucitya* or propriety clearly attempted to prevent all the subversive practices and representational aberrations from sneaking into the realm of literature.

Before I proceed further with these questions, I would like to make a caveat with respect to the scope of the current study. This chapter aims to explore only the ways in which *kāvyaśāstra* endeavoured to imbue Sanskrit *kāvya* with a deontic function. While it is true that Sanskrit *kāvya* generally adhered to the concept of *dharmavidhi* (moral injections prescribed in *śāstra*s) and instances where it deviated from this notion were rare, I do not wish to conclusively argue that Sanskrit *kāvya* always conformed to the notion of *dharmavidhi* set by *kāvyaśāstra* (literary theory) and never produced anything morally deviant. I refrain from making this claim because it is an endeavour that demands a fresh enquiry which lies beyond the scope of the current work.

Aucitya and the Rules of Representation

The Sanskrit word *aucitya* can literally be translated into English as 'propriety'. To put it in Foucauldian terminology, propriety—the standards of behaviour that are conventionally considered acceptable in any society—is essentially a set of 'discourses' governing our actions.[2] To control and condition subjects, there are so many 'discourses' or rules of propriety in any society. For example, there are discourses which dictate to us how we should behave in a public space, how we should address our elders, how a research paper has to be written, etc. What gets accepted as *aucitya* or propriety in a society is always the interest of the dominant group. By way of putting down the accepted practices in society, *aucitya* establishes what is called 'a regime of truth' (Foucault 1980: 131) or the notion of right and wrong in any society. Not only does propriety establish a regime of truth but it also assumes that all members of society adhere to these principles.

The concept of *aucitya* came to function as a critical standard in literary judgement at a relatively early date. Although it was developed as an independent category of theoretical investigation only in the 11th century Kṣemendra's *Aucityavicāracarcā aucitya* was already regarded as 'an all-embracing category of fitness, the life force pervading the limbs of a literary text, in regulating the use of everything from particular preverbs, particles, and individual words . . . to figures of speech, aesthetic moods (*rása*), and the argument of the work as a whole' (Pollock 2006: 198).[3]

A review of some major texts that became landmarks in the intellectual history of Sanskrit *kāvyaśāstra* will underscore the significance of *aucitya* in Sanskrit poetics. As in the case of many other concepts in Sanskrit poetics, the traces of concern for *aucitya* can be found as early as Bharata's *Nāṭyaśāstra*. When Bharata says that the characters should wear costumes according to their age, should walk according to their costume and should speak according to their gait, he is implicitly stating that one should be attentive to the idea of *aucitya* (1997: XIV.62). Ānandavardhana (9th century), probably the first literary theoretician to reflect systematically upon the concept of *aucitya*, says,

> A poet who follows the system of Bharata and others, who studies the work of great poets of the past, and who gives rein to his own genius, must be attentive and exert the greatest care not to relax or depart from the proprieties of the *vibhāvas* and other factors of *rasa*. (1990: 3.10–14 c)

Even Mahimabhaṭṭa, who wrote his seminal book *Vyaktiviveka* to challenge Ānanda's theory of *dhvani*, wholeheartedly concurred with the latter on the matter of *aucitya*. He did so by directly incorporating Ānanda's observations on *aucitya* from *Dhvanyāloka* into his own work. For Mahimabhaṭṭa, 'Composing a work in conformity with propriety is the very *Upaniṣad* of *rasa*' (1901: 31).

In *Vakroktijīvita*, Kuntaka also sees *aucitya* as a poetic merit and insists that a poet should pay due attention to it during the course of writing (1977: 193). Kuntaka's discussion of the idea of *aucitya* is primarily in connection with his criticism of Udbhaṭa's argument that *ūrjasvin*—the indecorous representation of *rasa*s and *bhāva*s—is a figure of speech. Kuntaka does not subscribe to Udbhaṭa's view that *ūrjasvin* is an *alaṅkāra*, since it tampers with the propriety of the period (402). He observes that *rasa*s, *bhāva*s, etc., that are bound together in an improper (*anaucitya*) fashion not only impede the improvement of *rasa* but also spoil it all together (404). He asks how a *rasa* marred by impropriety can shine forth as an ornament (405). In the third chapter of *Vakroktijīvita*, Kuntaka repeats Ānandavardhana and Mahimabhaṭṭa's stance that *aucitya* is the *Upaniṣad* of *rasa* and the spoiling of *rasa* is caused solely by the breach of propriety (404). In *Kāvyaprakāśa*, Mammaṭa warns poets against impropriety by saying that impropriety or *anaucitya* results in the aberration of emotion (*rasābhāṣa*) (1977: 72).

The 10th-century literary critic Bhoja was concerned about the moral ethos of his time even in the composition of his voluminous treatise on literary science *Śṛṅgāraprakāśa*. In the seventh chapter of *Śṛṅgāraprakāśa*, Bhoja declares, 'I hereby pray to the omnipotent God to help me ensure that while I am composing this book, there would be no transgression of the established order, the practice of the social orders and the four life stages' (1955: 257). Bhoja further elaborates on the importance of *aucitya* in the following verse from *Śṛṅgāraprakāśa*:

> Words suitable to each character
> Characters befitting the whole story
> The culmination of *rasa* at the right time and no deviation from the story line; a neat organization of component parts and the incorporation of suitable words.

> These are the virtues which will win attention of the erudite audience. (1963: 461)

In his *Sarasvatīkaṇṭhābharaṇa*, Bhoja talks about six kinds of *aucitya*s such as *viṣayaucitya* (propriety of subject), *vācyaucitya* (propriety of speech), *deśaucitya* (propriety of place), *samayaucitya* (propriety of time), *vaktrviṣayaucitya* (propriety of using language according to the status of the speaker) and *arthaucitya* (propriety in the use of language according to the subject matter) (1934: 942–949).

Kṣemendra, the 11th-century Sanskrit theoretician who made the concept of *aucitya* a separate body of knowledge in literary science, sees *aucitya* as the eternal life force of *kāvya* (*sthiramaninaśvaraṃ jīvitam kāvyasya*) (1954: 118). He compares a poem that does not conform to the standards of propriety to an unruly person who has worn ornaments in improper places and has consequently become a butt of ridicule. Kṣemendra says,

> An embellishment is a (real) embellishment if applied at the proper place; merits are always (real) merits when they are not divested of propriety. Put at a proper place, ornaments could beautify, otherwise they do not even deserve to be called ornaments. Similarly merits, if they do not fall short of propriety, are merits, otherwise they are blemishes. Who does not suffer mockery by (putting on) the girdle-string around the neck, the radiant necklace around the waist, the anklets on hands, the bracelets on feet, and (by showing) might against the prostrated and compassion towards foes? Similarly neither figures of speech nor the merits look charming without propriety. (135)

Bhānudatta in his *Rasataraṅgiṇī* states that '[i]mpropriety must by all means be carefully avoided' (2009: 329). Even the literary theoreticians who did not explicitly dealt with the concept of *aucitya* in their treatises emphasised the importance of *aucitya* in literature through their discussion of *kāvya doṣa*s—the improper elements in literature that can ruin the beauty of *kāvya*.[4] All these observations show that in the tradition of Sanskrit *kāvyaśāstra*, the notion of *aucitya* was a central concern.

It should also be borne in mind that *anaucitya* or impropriety was not absolutely unacceptable in *kāvya*. In the case of degenerate characters (*adhamā*), children and mentally deranged people, impropriety was very much acceptable. Creative writers often employed the impropriety of the inferior characters (*adhamā*) as a way to juxtapose them against the law-abiding noble characters (*uttamā*). Scholars as early as Bhāmaha had pointed out that *anaucitya* or impropriety is not a *nityadoṣa* or eternal blemish. Bhāmaha's discussion in this respect happens in chapter four of his *Kāvyālaṅkāra* where he discusses the *kāvyadoṣa* called *punarukti* or tautology. Creative writers and literary theoreticians generally consider *punarukti* as a *doṣa* since it results in boredom. But Bhāmaha points out that although *punarukti* is usually considered a poetic fault, it is very much acceptable in the representation of emotions such as fear, jealousy, etc. (1998: IV.14). Daṇḍin who holds the same view in *Kāvyālaṅkāra* shows how *doṣa*s turn out to be *guṇa*s in different situations. For example, *apārtha* or incoherent argument is generally considered a poetic fault. But it becomes a *guṇa* or poetic merit in portraying the raving of a madman or a child's prattle or the speech of a person who is sick (1962: IV.5–7). According to him, there are *vyabhicāra*s or exceptions to all the *doṣa*s (IV.5–7). Nāmisādhu, in his commentary on Rudraṭa's *Kāvyālaṅkāra*, explains this point further. He says that when one portrays a character who is not erudite or cultured, all the poetic faults turn out to be poetic merits. To explain his point, he cites the instance of the funny description of the illiterate husband of the poetess Vikaṭanitambā who is unable to pronounce words correctly (1886: 39). Pollock's observation in this regard merits attention here. He says that the presence of impropriety 'as such does not enfeeble literature, as if, since "the sole aim of literature" is *rasa*, when "real *rasa*" is not present, the true aim of literature is not attained. How, after all, could one have the *Rāmāyaṇa* without Rāvaṇa?' (2001: 211).

At this point, it is also important to mention that while the definition of proper behaviour may have evolved with changing times, the commitment to the concept of *aucitya* in *kāvyaśāstra* remained steadfast and unchanged. The changed notion of decorum was always meticulously incorporated in *kāvyaśāstra*. A case in point is the observation of Jagannātha about the polyandry of Draupadī. According to the ancient scholars who followed the old order of propriety, Draupadī having five husbands was not an act of impropriety. But Jagannātha opines that it is a clear case of social impropriety (1888: 101). In this passage, Jagannātha highlights the enduring significance of the concept of *aucitya* within *kāvyaśāstra*, despite the changing definitions of proper behaviour over time. This shows that *kāvyaśāstra* consistently adapted to evolving notions of social decorum.

Aucitya and the Two Methods

In *kāvyaśāstra*, the concept of *aucitya* functioned in two ways—first, through the prescription of the models for the representation of character types and emotions, and second, through the removal of improper situations from the already existing well-known stories. The tendency to prescribe the ideal models for the representation of character types and emotions starts from Bharata's *Nāṭyaśāstra* onwards.[5] On the basis of the degree to which a character conforms to the notion of propriety, Bharata divides the whole realm of character types into three broad categories, namely *uttamā* (the noble), *madhyamā* (the middling) and *adhamā* (the inferior) (1997: XXXIV). The characters belonging to the *uttamā* category always conform to the notion of *aucitya*; the second, that is the *madhyamā* category, occasionally lapses into *anaucitya*, and the *adhamā* characters never pay heed to *aucitya*. In the sixth chapter of *Nāṭyaśāstra*, Bharata talks about the ideal manner in which each category behaves. For instance, Bharata says that in the expression of *hāsya rasa* (the comic emotion), the noble characters (*uttamā*) always resort to only open laughter (*vihasita*) and smile (*smita*). The middling characters (*madhyamā*) express it through open laughter (*vihasita*) and laughter of ridicule (*upahasitam*). The inferior (*adhamā*) characters always resort to obscene (*apahasita*) and boisterous laughter (*atihasita*) (VI.64). Bharata's exposition likewise extends to other emotions, paying minute attention to even the movements of eyebrows. Another similar case in point is Bharata's description of three kinds of women—*uttamā*, *madhyamā* and *adhamā*—in conjunction with their conformity to the idea of propriety. According to Bharata, a *uttamā* female character is always unperturbed even in the face of unpleasant events. She does not speak harshly to her lover, does not retain her anger for long and does not conceal her mistakes. Being compliant with the dominant social order, she is always desired by men. A *madhyamā* female character, on the other hand, is always short-tempered, reciprocates the love of whoever loves her, is jealous of her rivals in love and is good at the art of lovemaking. An *adhamā* woman's character is always at war with the general conception of how an ideal woman should behave. A woman belonging to the *adhamā* category will express her anger without thinking about the propriety of place and time; she will not conform to the code of conduct and will always be harsh and proud (XXV.24). Bharata's dictum is that a creative writer should unfailingly and appropriately ascribe these qualities to each character type, as s/he represents them. In other words, a creative writer cannot represent a *uttamā* character with the qualities of an *adhamā* character and vice versa.[6]

Among all these models of character types that Bharata had developed, the most important one is his description of eight kinds of heroines (*aṣṭanāyikāḥ*) in eight different moods of which he talks in the 34th chapter of *Nāṭyaśāstra*. I consider this category particularly important because it became an imitable model of representation for many writers of *kāvya* and *kāvyaśāstra* in the subsequent centuries. These eight categories of women that Bharata mentions include *vāsakasajjā* (the heroine who is ready to meet her lover), *virahotkhaṇṭhitā* (the heroine whose husband is away from her), *svādhīnabhartṛkā* (the heroine whose lover is captivated by another woman), *kalahāntaritā* (the heroine whose lover got separated from her after a quarrel), *khaṇḍitā* (the heroine whose husband is enamoured by another woman), *vipralabdhā* (the heroine whose lover has broken his promise on a tryst), *proṣitabhartṛkā* (the heroine whose lover is abroad on an important mission) and *abhisārikā* (the heroine who indecorously runs after her lover) (1997: XXIV.184–191). Bharata gives a detailed mandate as to how each of these heroines should be represented in various situations. For instance, let us see how *abhisārikā* of libertine, noble, and maid varieties should behave during their tryst with their lovers. Bharata says,

> Whether a courtesan or a noble born, or a maidservant, a woman when an *abhisārikā* should act as follows: If a courtesan, she must deck herself with various ornaments, and, in the company of her servants, must walk slowly. If a highborn lady, she could cover herself with a veil and walk timidly and with downcast eyes in a lurking manner. If a maidservant, she should walk with uneven steps, her eyes beaming with joy, gesturing and babbling under the influence of intoxication. If the lover is in bed and asleep, she should awaken him in the following manner: A highborn lady should awaken him with the sound of ornaments, a courtesan by her scents and a maidservant by fanning him with her clothes. (XXIV.195–201)

These directives as to how different character types should behave are not limited to these eight heroines. It covers a wide range of areas such as how a scene of lovemaking should be depicted (1999: XXV.45–52); how different kinds of heroines should negotiate with their guilty lovers (XXIV.243–255); how male characters with different character traits such as *catura* (clever), *uttamā* (noble), *madhyamā* (middling character), *adhamā* (degenerate or low-born) and *saṃbravrttaka* (a lover who is indifferent to fear and anger) should behave in front of a courtesan (XXV.36–44); how the friend of a lover should act

(XXV.5–6) and so on. This tendency of setting appropriate models for the representation of different character types and aesthetic emotions runs through the length and breadth of the entire *kāvyaśāstra* tradition. Also, setting the right models of representation is not limited to Bharata's *Nāṭyaśastra*. Dhanañjaya's *Daśarūpaka*, Bhānudatta's *Rasamañjarī* and *Rasataraṅgiṇī*, Vidyānātha's *Pratāparudrīya* and Bhoja's *Śṛṅgāraprakāśa* are a few other texts that give directives in this manner.[7] It is significant to note that even if the writers of *kāvyaśāstra* did not elaborate on the specific representation of character types and emotions, it was clear from their emphasis on the idea of *aucitya* (as we saw before) that representational aberrations were not allowed in literature. In other words, the silence on the part of the literary theoreticians on the question of *aucitya* or their exiguous description of this category did not mean that they relaxed the importance of propriety. Many theoreticians often encouraged creative writers to look up *Nāṭyaśāstra* in case they had any doubts on the question of propriety.

Closely related to this tendency of setting models for each character type and aesthetic emotion was the elimination of situations (usually from a well-known plot) where an otherwise noble character commits an occasional act of impropriety. In *Vakroktijīvita*, Kuntaka refers to such emendations of plots. One such example that Kuntaka gives is the emendation of the plot done by Māyurāja in his drama *Udāttarāghava*. Kuntaka says that in the *Rāmāyaṇa*, it is Rāma's younger brother Lakṣmaṇa who goes in search of Rāma upon hearing the cry of the latter who has gone to catch the golden deer at the behest of Sitā. But in the drama *Udāttarāghava* by Māyurāja, the plot is rewritten in such a way that it is Rāma who goes to rescue Lakṣmaṇa. Such a revision of the plot was justified on the grounds that it is highly improper for a man of great prowess and courage like Rāma to be rescued by his younger brother Lakṣmaṇa (1977: 131).

Bhoja, in his *Śṛṅgāraprakāśa*, refers to a host of such incidents from the past where the poets rectified the occasional acts of impropriety committed by an otherwise *uttamā* character. A few such cases mentioned by Bhoja are worth mentioning here. Bhoja says that in the *Rāmāyaṇa*, it is Daśaratha, the king of Ayodhyā, who exiles his son Rāma to the forest to keep the word he has given to his wife Kaikeyī, Rāma's stepmother. But in the play *Nirdoṣadaśaratha*, this event is radically revised in such a way that Rāma is exiled not by Daśaratha and his wife Kaikeyī, but by two magical creatures who impersonate Daśaratha and Kaikeyī. In Bhavabhūti's *Mahāvīracarita*, Rāma has a fair duel with Vālin, as opposed to the original plot where Rāma treacherously kills Vālin by shooting an arrow at him from behind a tree. In the *Mahābhārata*, the noble character Bhīma drinks the blood of his enemy Duḥśāsana after killing him. Considering that such a heinous act is unbecoming of a high-born character like Bhīma, Bhaṭṭa Nārāyaṇa in his *Veṇīsaṃhāra*, revises this scene in such a way that Duḥśāsana's blood is drunk not by Bhīma, but by a demon who has possessed him. In *Harivaṃśa*, Māyāvatī is presented as the reincarnation of the wife of Kāma, the lord of love, and her lover Pradyumna as Kāma himself, in contrast to the original story where Pradyumna falls in love with Māyāvatī who is the wife of his preceptor. Such a change is made because *śṛṅgāra* with the guru's wife is socially unacceptable. In Kālidāsa's *Abhijñānaśākuntala*, Duṣyanta does not recognise Śakuntalā, not because Duṣyanta's love for Śakuntalā is inconsistent, but because Śakuntalā was cursed by sage Durvāsa that Duṣyanta would forget her. Yet another major work that Bhoja refers to in connection with the revision of the plot is *Calitarāma*. The play *Calitarāma* portrays Rāma's return to Ayodhyā after his victory over Rāvaṇa and recovery of his wife Sītā. But in the version of the story given in *Calitarāma*, Rāma spurns Sītā because he was deceived by a posse of his surviving enemies led by a demon named Lavaṇa. In Māyurāja's *Tāpasavatsarāja*, which is an emendation of Bhāsa's *Svapnavāsavadattā*, the minster lies to King Udayana that Queen

Vāsavadattā perished in the fire, not to conduct the marriage between Udayana and Padmavatī, but to save the king who is enamoured by Vāsavadattā to the point of neglecting his kingly duties (1963: 460).

It is significant to note that this effort to censor elements which are against the interests of the existing notions of propriety was applicable not only to the representation of emotions, character types and situations but to the very diction of *kāvya* as well. Literary theoreticians as early as Bhāmaha instruct the authors to avoid terms that are considered taboo. According to Bhāmaha, writers should always stay away from such faults as *śrutiduṣṭa* (offensive to ear), *arthaduṣṭa* (improper or objectionable meaning) and *kalpanāduṣṭa* (objectionable constructions wherein joining of words gives rise to an objectionable sense) (1998: I.47). Bhāmaha gives a list of words and expressions like *varcas* (excrement), *sambādha* (vagina), *thaṛṣita* (seduced/outraged), *dhaṛṣita* (vomiting) or *udgāra* (ejaculation) that are to be avoided (I.48). He is also very particular about the combination of words that can give rise to obscene meanings like '*sa śauryābharaṇḥ*' (I.52). Here the sentence means 'he whose ornament is valour'. Bhāmaha considers this sentence obscene because the sentence has the word '*yābh*' which is an indecorous term for sexual intercourse.

Daṇḍin also holds the same opinion. According to him, the expression—'Hey maiden, why don't you love me who loves you a lot?'—is *grāmya* (uncouth and unpolished), as it explicitly expresses a man's desire for a woman (1962: I.63). Such explicit expressions of sexual desire, says Daṇḍin, should strictly be avoided from *kāvya* because it generates obscenity. Daṇḍin is against any explicit representation of *saṃbhoga-śṛṅgāra* (love-in-union) and the employment of taboo terms referring to love-making (61).[8] Like Bhāmaha, Daṇḍin points out that a poet should always be careful about the conjoining of words in a sentence so that it does not give the readers an impression of a taboo word. He cites a few examples in this respect. For example, when we separately speak out each word in the sentence '*yā bhavataḥ priyā*', the sentence means 'whoever is the beloved of the lord'. But when we conjoin these words and speak rapidly, they undergo the process of elision, and come to mean 'the beloved of the one who is overly interested in love-making'. Similarly, the sentence *kharam prahṛtya viśrāntaḥ puruṣo vīryavāniti* means 'having struck [the demon] Khara the heroic personage [Rama] is taking his rest'. But, because of the double entendre of the words here, it can denote an obscene signification—'the virile youth [*viśrāntaḥ puruṣḥ*] is taking rest after thrashing [making love with his beloved]'. According to Daṇḍin, instances of obscenity, such as these, are always against the interest of propriety, and hence, should be summarily removed from literature. According to Vāmana, a word should be completely avoided from the entire gamut of *kāvya*, even if only one of its significations is obscene. A word that Vāmana cites as an example of this is *varcaḥ*. The term *varcaḥ* simultaneously means 'glorious' and 'excrement'. Since the word is popularly considered a taboo term to denote human excreta, Vāmana holds that it should not be used in poetry. He goes on to argue that even words that are phonetically similar to a taboo word should be censored (1962: II.1.15–20).

Aucitya and *Kaviśikṣā*

According to scholars like Pollock, Sanskrit *kāvya* tradition for the most part did not veer away from the generally accepted representation of character types and situations. It encouraged typicality and did not usually pose resistance to the dominant worldview of society. Pollock observes,

> Sanskrit poets were interested in exploring typicality and, accordingly needed to master it across the whole universe of emotion. How were women expected to act when first falling in love, when confronted by an act of infidelity on the part of their lovers, when desiring someone other than their husband? To answer such questions a discourse arose

> that aimed to construct a typology of character. (2001: Introduction to *Bouquet of Rasa*, xxxiii)

This typicality in the representation of character types and situations was maintained throughout the history of the Sanskrit *kāvya* tradition primarily through the process of *kaviśikṣā* or the formal training of poets. Formal education in the art of composing literature was compulsory in the *kāvyaśāstra* tradition in Sanskrit. The exponents of *kāvyaśāstra* propagated the view that a *kavi*, even if he was naturally endowed with the talent of composing poems, would remain incomplete as a creative writer in the absence of proper training (*śikṣā*). Thus *kavi* was made to undergo a conditioning process before the production of *kāvya*. It is a truism that *pratibhā* or inborn genius was often privileged over *vyutppatti* or training. But *vyutppatti* was indeed an unavoidable element in the establishment of a poet.

Writers from Bhāmaha onwards talk about the importance of formal training in *kāvya*. Bhāmaha opines that the desire to compose *kāvya*s could be entertained only after mastering all *śāstra*s necessary for the composition of literature (1998: I.10). Daṇḍin is of the view that just as a blind person is incapable of differentiating between different colours, so also a poet devoid of training cannot distinguish between poetic merits and excellence (1962: I.8). He observes that even if a person falls short of *pratibhā*, s/he can excel in the art of composing *kāvya* through sheer training (I.104).

Vāmana is of the view that an aspiring poet should get trained in literary science to distinguish between poetic merits and faults. As far as he is concerned, even if one is naturally endowed with poetic genius, he should definitely undergo formal training before writing *kāvya*s (2000: I.1–4–5). According to Mammaṭa, *kāvya* is the result of 'knowledge born of a study of the world, of sciences and of poems, and the practice of the teachings of those versed in writing poetry' (1966: I.3). Jayadeva opines that just as the cause of the creeper is water and seed, so also the poetry is the result of *pratibhā* (inborn genius), *vyutpatti* (training) and *abhyāsa* (practice) (1932: I.6). In his

Kāvyamīmāṃsā, Rājaśekhara says, 'The prior knowledge of *śāstra* is essential for an appreciation of *kāvya*. Just as nothing is visible in the dark without the aid of light, so also no poet can create without knowledge of *śāstra*' (2000: 20). In *Sāhityamīmāṃsā*, Maṅkha says that a *kavi* should be endowed with three essential prerequisites such as *śruta* (instruction), *abhiyoga* (practice) and *pratibhāśakti* (poetic genius) (1984: 118). All these testify that one was not born a poet, but made a poet through training.

It should be noted that learning of rhetoric and prosody (although it was very important) was only one of the many aspects of *kaviśikṣā*. It also included the learning of knowledge from other fields of knowledge such as *kāmaśāstra* (theory of erotics), *arthaśāstra* (theory of politics), *mokṣaśāstra* (theory of salvation), etc. that codified the idea of 'propriety' in various fields of knowledge in day-to-day life. Lienhard observes,

> Since they [poets] were expected to deal with things in a factual matter, the sciences that were closely allied in a narrow sense were not enough and a knowledge of numerous other fields was required, above all of erotics (*kāmaśāstra*), logic (*nyāya*), the arts (*kalā*), political science (*arthaśāstra*) and familiarity with such important sources of literary material as the epics the *Rāmāyaṇa* and *Mahābhārata* as well as with Purāṇas. (1984: 19)

It is no wonder, then, that a poet who underwent *kaviśikṣā* did not produce anything that challenged the propriety of the period.

Vāmana's observation about the importance of a poet conforming to the normalised truth claims of the society (recorded in the *śāstras*) typifies how *kaviśikṣā* functioned in preconditioning a poet in the way the dominant forces in the society desired. The *doṣa* (poetic fault) that he refers to as *vidyāvirudham* (opposition to [the dominant] knowledge systems) is clearly an attempt to condition the poet according to the dominant moral and social views. Vāmana opines that any representation of facts against what is written in the *śāstras* will be a blotch on *kāvya*. To demonstrate the poetic blemish called *vidyāvirudham* and warn the poet against it, Vāmana cites a few examples. According to *dharmaśāstra*, it is to restore justice that kings conquer the world. If a poet says that it is to satiate their material desires that kings win over countries, that will result in a poetic blemish. According to *Daṇḍaśāstranīti,* it is because of a person's prudent conduct and diplomacy that others succumb to him/her. But if somebody says that it is a person's aggressiveness that enables him to win over others, then it clashes with the socially accepted norm of *Daṇḍaśāstranīti* and consequently results in the poetic blemish of contradicting *caturvarga-śāstra*. Similarly, according to *Kāmaśāstra*, the lower lip (*adhara*) is the right place to kiss, not the upper lip (*uttaroṣṭha*). Contrary to this dictum in *Kāmaśāstra*, if a poet states that the upper lip is the right place to kiss, the poet will court a poetic blemish. Vāmana's injunction that a poet should always pay heed to these *śāstra*s which draw a neat line between what is acceptable and unacceptable within a social framework is something which runs through the whole system of Sanskrit poetics like a red thread. Similar observations are made by theoreticians like Bhāmaha, Daṇḍin, Mammaṭa and so on.[9]

This implies that a poet who got trained in the *kāvyaśāstra* was thus encouraged to produce literary artefacts in the way the dominant group in society preferred. We can undoubtedly say that this pedagogical practice always served as an effective tool in the Sanskrit literary circle to make creative writers compliant and suppress any deviant representation of character types and emotions. This kind of prescriptivism not only suppressed the emergence of alternative ideologies but also predetermined the nature of character types and their actions even before a *kāvya* was actually composed. In other words, even though the name and the local habitation of the characters and the objects changed from *kāvya* to *kāvya*, their representation was predetermined by the laws of propriety. By its insistence on the 'suitability' of all aspects of literature, from the word to character traits, *aucitya* pre-empted any attempt in Sanskrit literary tradition to pose resistance to the truth claims endorsed by the dominant power structure.

To put it in contemporary sociological terminology, *kaviśikṣā* functioned as a soft power which aimed to 'affect others to obtain preferred outcome by co-option and attraction rather than coercion' (Nye 2010: 216). Soft power structures the behaviour and interests of the dominated class in consistency with the preferences of the dominant class, not through physical coercion, but through cultural and ideological tools and institutions. By propagating the idea that conformity to *aucitya* or propriety is necessary to compose an excellent *kāvya* and become a creative writer par excellence, the dominant class in society won over the creative writers to produce literary works in tune with its interest. The poets who were under the sway of the soft power of the dominant class willingly self-censored themselves and conformed to the stereotypical notions of representation prevalent in society.

Kāvya and the Symbolic Power

Sanskrit *kāvyasāstra* in conjunction with the theory of *aucitya* aimed to precondition the representation of character types and situations in *kāvya* in compliance with the interest of the dominant groups because *kāvya* functioned as a tool to socially condition the readers in accordance with the rules of *puruṣārtha*s. The term *puruṣārtha* refers to the teachings on the four goals of life such as *dharma* (righteousness), *artha* (wealth), *kāma* (pleasure) and *mokṣa* (salvation). *Dharma* aims to teach duties, rights, laws, code of conduct and the right way of living; *artha* is concerned with the proper pursuit of wealth; *kāma* relates to the right way of indulging in pleasure, both sensual and sexual, and *mokṣa* takes up the question of activities that a person should necessarily need to perform to attain liberation. Sanskrit literary theorists as far back as Bharata believed that *kāvya* also had a deontic function, in addition to its primary function of aesthetic pleasure. Bharata's reference to the context, in which Brahmā created *nāṭya*, can be considered one of the earliest references to the didactic function of art in India. In response to the sage's query regarding the origin of drama, Bharata says that Brahmā created *nāṭya* to enlighten the morally degenerate people (belonging to all castes) of *tretāyuga* (the age of triads). Bharata says that when *tretāyuga* began, the entire world became corrupt and people started following what he calls *grāmya-dharma* or indecorous lifestyle. At this juncture, the gods approached Brahmā and asked him to create a new *Veda* so that people of all castes could become righteous. Thus, at the behest of gods, Brahmā created *nāṭya* as a tool of didacticism (1997: I.6). Brahmā's declaration about the function of *nāṭya*, reported by Bharata in *Nāṭyaśāstra*, is worth exploring here. Brahmā says that *nāṭya* which is based on the actions of three kinds of human beings—namely *uttamā* (the noble), *madhyamā* (the middling) and *adhamā* (the inferior)—aims to instruct the spectators of all time about everything in the world. Quoting Brahmā's words, Bharata says that *nāṭya* came into being to instruct men (*lokopadeśajananam nāṭyametad bhaviṣyati*) (I.86). Bharata's is not an isolated observation in this regard. To show the didactic function implicit in art, Bhaṭṭa Tauta, as recorded by Abhinavagupta in his *Locana*, draws an interesting analogy between *rasa*, drama and the *Veda*. According to Tauta: 'Rasa is the delight; delight is the drama; and drama is the Veda' (1990: 3:10–14 f L).

Bhāmaha, who is considered the founding father of *kāvyaśāstra* in Sanskrit, also shares the opinion of Bharata. According to Bhāmaha, 'Composition of good poetry produces ability in (or makes one able, or capable in the pursuit of) *dharma*, *artha*, *kāma* and *mokṣa*' (1998: I.2.4). In his commentary upon Udbhaṭa's *Kāvyālaṅkāra-sāra-saṃgraha*, Pratihārendurāja opines that *rasa* is a source of instruction

(1982: 53). Rudraṭa *in Kāvyālaṅkāra* even privileges the deontic function of *kāvya* over its aesthetic function. He says,

> Does not the knowledge of *dharma* (righteousness), *artha* (wealth), *kāma* (joy), and *mokṣa* (salvation) reach sensitive minds easily and pleasingly through poetry? People are always weary of *śāstras*. Therefore poetry contains *rasa* to serve the purpose of *śāstras* in a joyous manner. (1886: XII.1–2)

Abhinavagupta in his *Locana* on Ānanda's *Dhvanyāloka* says that the study of good poetry gives readers knowledge in *dharma, artha, kāma* and *mokṣa* (1990: 71). In *Vakroktijīvita*, Kuntaka also sees *rasa* as a means to instruct readers about the four aims of life in a way that is conspicuously distinct from *śāstra, purāṇas* and the *Veda* (1977: I.5). In *Kāvyaprakāśa*, Mammaṭa also holds the same opinion: 'Poetry brings fame and riches, knowledge of the ways of the world and relief from evils, and counsel sweet as from the lips of a beloved consort' (1966: I.2). In *Sāhityadarpaṇa*, Viśvanātha opines that even a dumbhead will be morally enlightened through the consumption of *kāvya*. He says,

> Since the attainment of the fruits consisting of the class of four, i.e., the four great objects of human desire—viz., Merit, Wealth, Enjoyment and Liberation is pleasantly possible even in the case of those of slender capacity, by means of poetry only, therefore its nature shall be now set forth. (I.2)

In *Śṛṅgāraprakāśa*, Bhoja also declares, 'A literary artefact should be understood as a combination of sentences that informs us as to what we should do and should not do' (1955: 120).

What we specifically need to note here is that the deontic function that *kāvya* performed was entirely different from that of the *Vedas* and *śāstras*. Kuntaka's position in this regard is worth mentioning here. He opines that while the *śāstra* and the other allied disciplines talk about the moral duties incumbent upon them in an insipid way, *kāvya* performs the same function in a pleasurable manner. Kuntaka says,

> Literary artefacts such as *mahākāvya* create pleasure in the nobles. Noble persons like princes are supposed to learn the aims of life such as *dharma*. But being fickle and joyous by nature, they are reluctant to make an effort to learn them. *Kāvya* will be like a toy to them. Therefore they can learn *dharma* of life in a pleasurable way. (1977: I.3)

According to Abhinavagupta, while *kāvya* implicitly 'instructs after the fashion of a wife', the *Veda*s explicitly 'instruct after the fashion of a master' (1990: 71). To put it in other words, Abhinavagupta says that while *kāvya* pleasingly and implicitly instructs the readers, the *Veda*s and *śāstra*s explicitly inform the readers as to how they should function in society. According to Abhinava, *rasa* is a sugar-coated pill for young princes who are neither educated in scriptures nor have received any instruction from history. Abhinava observes:

> Princes who are not educated in Scripture—those words of *śruti* and *smṛti* which consists in commands like those of a master to do this or that—and who have not received instruction from history, which like a friend reveals to us the connection of cause and effect with such persuasive instances like 'this result came from such an act,' and who are therefore in pressing need of instruction for they, given the power to accomplish the wants of their subjects, can be given instruction in the four goals of man only by our entering into their hearts. And what enters into the heart is the relish of *rasa* (*rasasvada*, the imaginative experience of emotion). Now, since this rasa is brought about by the union of the *vibhāva*s and their related factors, a union which is invariably connected with instruction in the four goals of man, it follows that the subjection of a man to the relishing of the rasas by a literary construction of the *vibhāva*s, etc., appropriate to *rasa*, serves at the same time for the instruction (*vyutpatti*) that naturally results. In this way [literary] delight (*pratiti*) is an aid to instruction. (1990: 437)

The crux of Abhinavagupta's dictum is that while *śāstra* and the *Veda*s explicitly give moral instruction to readers, *kāvya* performed its deontic function rather implicitly through suggestion. Mammaṭa also reproduces the same quotation in *Kāvyaprakāśa* while talking about the way in which *kāvya* instructs its readers (1966: 2–3).

This observation gives rise to another question: How did *kāvya* perform its deontic function implicitly? Sanskrit literary theoreticians have given a theoretical explanation for this. According to them, *kāvya* exercised this deontic function obliquely by presenting noble characters (who always conform to *dharmavidhi*) perpetually emerging victorious and the indecorous *adharmic* characters always perishing in their lives. While the victory of the noble characters inspired readers to conform to *dharmavidhi*, the fall of the indecorous or *adhamā* characters made them repulsive towards any actions that go against the existing notions of *dharma*.

One of the first literary theoreticians to comment upon this reader-oriented didactic function of *kāvya* was Kuntaka. In *Vakroktijīvita*, Kuntaka talks about the process of readers self-fashioning themselves after the noble heroes in *kāvya* who follow *dharmavidhi* or the moral action prescribed by society. According to Kuntaka,

> In the *Rāmāyaṇa*-based dramas of great poets which shine forth with all the five figurative deviations, what we have on the surface is the description of the noble heroes. But in reality, it ends up in a moral injunction—'act like Rama, not like Rāvaṇa.' Similarly, in *Tāpasavatsarāja*, the surface meaning denotes the history of the 'flower-hearted' hero who is immersed in lovely games. But in reality, it advises [indirectly] that it is incumbent upon a minister to save his king who is drowning in the sea of sorrow. (1977: 132–133)

Abhinavagupta in his *Locana* on Ānandavardhana's *Dhvanyāloka* also echoes the same observation. He observes,

> We further admit that the educative effect (*vyutpādana*) [of poetry] is different from that which comes from scripture through its mandates and from history through its narrations. For in addition to the analogy which it furnishes that we should behave like *Rāma* [and not like Rāvaṇa], it produces in the final result an expansion

> of one's imagination which serves as the means of tasting the *rasas*. (1990: 2.4 L)

In his *Sāhityadarpaṇa*, Viśvanātha makes a similar observation. According to Viśvanātha, a reader who is desirous of achieving the four ends of human life should always model himself or herself upon the ideal characters of *kāvya*: 'To attain the four ends of human life from *kāvya*, one should act like Rāma and not like Rāvaṇa' (2016: 2).

In *Kāvyaprakāśa*, Mammaṭa also subscribes to the view that *kāvya* instructs the readers about the four goals of life indirectly and pleasingly. Mammaṭa observes,

> Such poetry is the work of poets, clever in depicting things in a manner passing the comprehension of ordinary men. It offers to other poets and cultured men counsel most persuasively, by means of a moving tenderness in the manner of it (that is, in the words)—counsel such as that one should behave like Rāma and not like Rāvaṇa. As such, poetry is by all means to be studied and cultivated. (1966: I.2)

Bhoja also makes a similar observation in *Śṛṅgāraprakāśa*. He explains at length how readers need to read *kāvya* and self-fashion themselves after the characters who abide by the rules of decorum prevalent in society (1955: 479). This notion of Sanskrit literary theoreticians about the 'uses' of stories in *kāvya* is in line with Plato's concept of poetry as a sugar-coated pill that the readers should necessarily fashion themselves after the image of the noble characters portrayed in *kāvya*. While *śāstra*, *itihāsa* and the *Veda* explicitly inform their readers as to how to behave, *kāvya* coaxes its readers into modelling their subjectivity after the noble characters who conform to the mores and values of society.[10]

To make literature an implicit tool of moral education, *kāvyaśāstra* always insisted that literature should never fail to create aspiration for a morally upright lifestyle. For this, literary theoreticians insisted that *kāvya* should always show the ultimate victory of the characters who conform to social decorum and the decay of those who defy it. Bhoja says that *kāvya* should never show that a law-abiding noble character, despite conforming to the rules of decorum, fails to emerge victorious over a law-breaking *adhamā* character. If there is an instance which is contrary to this in a story, the poet should make it a point to rewrite the story in such a way that the law-abiding moral character prevails and the wrong-doing *adhamā* character perishes. Bhoja says:

> If a person desires to compose a literary work based on a plot from the epics, it is possible that a character who conforms to propriety might not only fail to attain the desired result, but also might receive what he does not desire. On the other hand, another character who has no regard for propriety might attain the result he desires. In such cases, the plot must be revised in such a way that the character who conforms to propriety is not denied the result he desires, and the other person should not only fail to attain his desire, but also should attain what he does not want. (1934: II.481)

The victory of the characters who live according to the laws of *aucitya* and the decay of those who defy them definitely create aspiration among the readers of *kāvya* to emulate the propriety-bound ways and manners of the noble characters.

The conception in the Sanskrit cosmopolis of a poet as a prophet or seer further strengthened the 'symbolic power' of *kāvya* by way of earning the reader's trust in whatever the *kavi* spoke. The term '*kavi*' was originally employed to refer to the Vedic hymnists to whom the *Veda*s were revealed in endless time, without beginning or end. The idea of the poet as a seer with a prophetic vision, in fact, begins with the *Rāmāyaṇa* where the omniscient narrator says that the whole story of Rāma appeared to Vālmīki in a prophetic vision during his composition of the *Rāmāyaṇa*: '*tataḥ paśyati dharmātmā tat sarvaṅ yōgamāsthitaḥ / purā yattatra nirvṛttam pāṇāvāmalakam yathā*' (With the power of yoga, the righteous [Vālmīki] saw clearly, like an *amalaka* fruit in the palm of the hand, the entire course of events that happened in the past relating to Rāma) (I.3.6).

In *Kāvyānuśāsana*, Hemacandra equates the poet with a prophet and says that one who is not a seer is not a poet (1964: 369).

The image of a poet as a seer or prophet in fact cuts across various cultures in early Indian societies, and it invariably became indispensable in the validation of political power. The king-as-patron always employed the poet to reel off eulogies (*stuti*s) or compose elaborate genealogies (*vamsavali*s) to position him in a reputed and fabulous dynasty (2000: 167). Thapar points out how the bard or *sūta*, despite his lower caste, 'was often seen as outside the normal hierarchy of caste and, at the same time, evolved a ritual which gave him a special sanction' (2000: 39). Upinder Singh observes a similar pattern in early South India: 'The most important basis of legitimation of political power in early historical South India was the eulogy of the poets' (432). Besides, this was the high social status of the *kavi* or poet: 'The social position of the poet in ancient India was a very honoured one. The poet enjoyed a highly privileged and enviable status in the assemblies and concourses of the cultured classes in those days' (Krishnamoorthy 1964: 167). This shows that the dominant social forces in society which coaxed the poet to produce *kāvya* in conformity with the rules of decorum managed to vindicate everything that the *kavi* presented by projecting him as a great visionary who could see the past, present and future with his divine vision. To the reader, the *kavi* (poet) became a demi-god who professed truths and values that had to be emulated.

Kāvyaśāstra contained within itself an inbuilt mechanism which made sure that the very act of writing eliminated everything that had the potential to dislodge the interest of the dominant class. Central to this mechanism was the idea of *aucitya* or propriety. The concept of *aucitya* functioned in Sanskrit *kāvyaśāstra* primarily through two mechanisms. First of all, it set models for the representation of character types, situations and emotions and encouraged the creative writer to follow those models keenly in the production of literary artefacts. And secondly, it gave the creative writers a clear mandate to censor those situations in which an otherwise morally upright character commits a breach of propriety. These two mechanisms, through which *aucitya* functioned, played a vital role in socially and aesthetically conditioning the creative writer to produce literary artefacts in complete compliance with the interest of the dominant power structure in society. It is interesting to note that *kaviśikṣā* (teaching of the poet) was a prerequisite of creative writing wherein the creative writers were pre-conditioned to produce the literary artefacts in complete conformity with the interest of the dominant class. Such a mechanism also prevented *kāvya* from challenging the taken-for-granted claims prevalent in society. This conditioning of the ontology of different character types and situations in *kāvya* through the theory of *aucitya* was ultimately a way to socially condition the readers of *kāvya*. By portraying the characters who act according to the norms of *aucitya* always emerging victorious and those who rebel with it failing, *kāvyaśāstra* preconditioned the ontology of *kāvya* in such a way that the readers will aspire to emulate morally upright noble characters and abhor the morally degenerate villains. Thus, Sanskrit *kāvyaśāstra* in conjunction with the concept of *aucitya* functioned as a censorship mechanism and a metanarrative on the ontology of literature to impose an ontological certitude upon the very form of *kāvya*.

4

Vakrokti as a Resistance to *Svabhāva*

This chapter focuses on the idea of *vakrokti* (deviant utterance), originally conceptualised by the 7th-century literary critic Bhāmaha in his *Kāvyālaṅkāra* and later explored in detail by the 10th-century critic Kuntaka in his text *Vakroktijīvita*. In this chapter, I argue that Kuntaka's concept of *vakrokti* is a 'transformative' act to enrich both the author and reader's range of aesthetic experience by pushing them out of their familiar structures of performance and perception. As opposed to the infinite enactment of the same old dominant structures, which results in a restricted form of thinking and acting, Kuntaka's theory of *vakrokti* aims to experiment with the existing structures—both linguistic and non-linguistic—so as to generate new structures hitherto untried. As far as Kuntaka is concerned, *svabhāvokti* or 'the act of depicting things in the way they are dominantly conceived' holds no place in the realm of *kāvya* (2009). He sees *kavi* as a 'transformative' or 'creative' agent who aims to shatter our ontological certitude about ideas and entities by presenting them in a hitherto unfamiliar fashion.

The text that is going to receive maximum attention in this chapter is Kuntaka's *Vakroktijīvita*. Nevertheless, to substantiate my point further, I also bank upon Bhāmaha's *Kāvyālaṅkāra*, Udbhaṭa's *Kāvyālaṅkāra-sāra-saṃgraha* as well as Ānandavardhana and Abhinavagupta's commentaries on Bhāmaha's key passages on *vakrokti* in *Kāvyālaṅkāra*. This chapter is organised into four sections. The first section offers a brief account of the idea of *vakrokti* before and after Kuntaka's *Vakroktijīvita*. This historical overview, I think, is necessary to highlight the importance of Kuntaka's treatment of *vakrokti* in the intellectual history of Sanskrit literary theory and also to justify my detailed exploration of this single text. The second and third sections, which constitute the crux of this chapter, examine how the idea of *vakrokti* challenges our adherence to habitual patterns of perception and performance, thereby facilitating a liberating experience for the reader, author and the entities that are being portrayed in a deviant manner. In light of these observations in the second and third sections, the fourth section problematises the concept of *vakrokti* vis-à-vis the figure of the reader who reads a *vakrokti-kāvya*.

The History of *Vakrokti*

In the realm of Sanskrit *kāvyaśāstra*, Bhāmaha is the first literary theoretician to use the term *vakrokti*.[1] He employed the term *vakrokti* in connection with his discussion of the figure of speech *atiśayokti*. According to Bhāmaha, *atiśayokti* is the treatment of an object or idea in such a way that it appears strikingly new to the readers. In other words, in the figure of speech called *atiśayokti*, an object or entity transcends our familiar equations of perceiving it. The following is an example of *atiśayokti* which Bhāmaha cites in *Kāvyālaṅkāra*: 'If the loose skin of water drops down like the slough of serpents, then it will become the white garments on the limbs of ladies sporting on in the water' (1998: II.83). In this example, Bhāmaha gives us a deviant (*vakratā*) and the hitherto unfamiliar equation of perceiving water. The dominant conception about water is that it is a colourless, odourless, liquid which forms water bodies, such as rivers, oceans, ponds and so on. But, by considering water as a white garb on the limbs of ladies playing in the water, Bhāmaha changed the dominant conception of water.

According to Bhāmaha, *atiśayokti* is identical to *vakrokti* (deviant utterance), and all poets should take special care to master this art of deviant utterance. In *Kāvyālaṅkāra*, Bhāmaha says, 'This [*atiśayokti*] is nothing but *vakrokti*. All meanings appear new by this. Poets should be assiduous in cultivating it. Where is an *alaṅkāra* without this?' (1998: I.85). Bhāmaha says that ordinary expressions, which reproduce the dominant way we perceive entities without any figurative deviation (*vakratā*), should not be considered an *alaṅkāra*, and the matter-of-fact expressions bereft of *vakratā* are mere *vārtā* (report), not *kāvya* (poetry). Bhāmaha observes, '"The sun has set; the moon shines, the birds are winging back to their nests." What kind of poetry is this? This is called *vārtā*' (II.87).[2] Holding *vakrokti* in high esteem, Bhāmaha is reluctant to consider *svabhāvokti*—the act of presenting something in the way it is commonly perceived—as an *alaṅkāra*. While describing the five kinds of *kāvya*, Bhāmaha reiterates that *kāvya*, in any form, becomes commendable, only if it is characterised by deviant utterance (*yukta vakṛasvabhāvoktyā sarvamevaitadiṣṭyate*; I.30). For him, a composition which is clear, smooth and elegant, but devoid of deviant utterance, will be mere music (not *kāvya*) (I.34).

According to Daṇḍin, the successor of Bhāmaha, the whole universe of speech can be divided into two, namely *vakrokti* and *svabhāvokti* (1962: II. 363). Vāmana holds that *vakrokti* is subsumed in 'the secondary usage based on similarity' (*sadrśya-lakṣaṇā-vakrokti)* and is just a *śabdālaṅkāra* (IV. 3.8). The first literary theoretician to use the term *vakrokti* as a separate poetic figure is the 9th-century Kashmiri critic Rudraṭa (Bronner and McCrea 2001: 439). As far as Rudraṭa is concerned, *vakrokti* is an *arthālaṅkāra* which can be divided into two broad categories, namely *śleṣa-vakrokti* and *kāku-vakrokti*.[3] Ānandavardhana, a contemporary of Rudraṭa in the court of King Avantivarman, also refers to the concept of *vakrokti* in his *Dhvanyāloka*. In the third *udyota* of *Dhvanyāloka*, Ānanda subscribes to Bhāmaha's opinion that *vakratā* which is identical with *atiśayokti* is the very life force of all *alaṅkāras*. Ānanda observes,

> All [hyperboles] are deviant utterances [*vakrokti*].
> By it meaning is exalted.
> A poet must take pains with it,
> [for] what is figure of speech without it. (1990: 602)

In *Dhvanyāloka*, Ānandavardhana further reaffirms the importance of *vakratā*, when he sarcastically talks about a fool's conception of a good *kāvya*.

Abhinava's commentary on this passage is also important in connection with our discussion of *vakrokti*. In his commentary, Abhinava opines that *vakratā* is identical with sublime *saṃghaṭanā* (*vakrokti ulkṛṣṭa saṃghaṭanā*) and the lack of *vakratā* means the absence of beauty. Abhinava says, '"Striking turn of speech" [*vakratā*]: elevated style or arrangement (*saṃghaṭanā*). That it lacks this implies that it lacks the qualities of sound and meaning' (1990: 1.1c *L*). Bhoja, in his *Śṛṅgāraprakāśa*, opines that there is no *kāvya* without *vakrokti*. He divides the whole universe of speech into *vacas* and *kāvya*. While *vacas*—the representation of objects and ideas in the way they are dominantly perceived or presented in daily life—is the hallmark of ordinary speech, *kāvya* is marked by *vakratā* or deviant utterance (1955: 221).

Mammaṭa in his *Kāvyaprakāśa* sees *vakrokti* in both its narrow and broad senses. In its narrow sense, the term *vakratā* is a category of *śabdālaṅkāra*. He says, 'When what is said by one person in one sense is construed by another person in a different sense—either through punning or through intonation—it is called equivoque (*vakrokti*)' (1966: 317). Like Rudraṭa, Mammaṭa also divides *vakrokti* into two categories of *śabdālaṅkāra*, namely, *śleṣa-vakrokti* and *kāku-vakrokti*. In its broadest sense, Mammaṭa sees *vakrokti* as the essence of all *alaṅkāras* by quoting Bhāmaha's dictum that is no *alaṅkāra* without *vakrokti* (1966: 458). Sharing the opinion of Mammaṭa, Ruyyaka sees *vakrokti* first as a category of *śabdālaṅkāra*, and later, as the life force of all *alaṅkāras* (228). He also divides *vakrokti* into *kāku-vakrokti* and *śleṣa-vakrokti* (227). For Viśvanātha (2016: 339) and Viśveśvara (1997: 145), *vakrokti* is a mere ornament of sound. Vidyānātha (1933: 297), Jayadeva (1932: 106), Appayya Dīkṣita (1903: 259), Purohita (1903: 259) and Amrtānandayogin (1949: 305–316) treat *vakrokti* as an *arthālaṅkāra*.

In *kāvya* tradition, the first major literary work that avowedly claims to make use of the possibilities of *vakrokti* is the 9th-century Kashmiri poet Ratnākara's *Vakroktipañcaśikā*. *Vakroktipañcaśikā* can be rightly called the most influential specimen of the nascent genre of *vakrokti* poetry (Bronner and McCrea 2001: 440).[4] Considering *vakrokti* as the ultimate locus of literariness in *kāvya*, many practising poets called themselves the erudite practitioners in the employment of *vakrokti*. For instance, the poet Kavirāja in his *Rāghavapāṇḍaviya* names himself, Subandhu and Bāṇabhaṭṭa as the only three experts in the employment of *vakrokti*. He asks: 'Subandhu, Bāṇa, and Kavirāja are the only three masters of deviant utterance. Can there be a fourth one?' (1987: 1.41). Later, in the early 13th century, Vidyāmādhava added his own name to this list and confidently declared that there could not be a fifth one. In his *Pārvatīrukmiṇīya*, a work modelled on Kavirāja's *Rāghavapāṇḍaviya*, Vidyāmādhava remarks: 'Bāṇa, Subandhu, Kavirāja and I, the erudite scholar Vidyāmādhava, are the only four masters of deviant utterance in this world. There will never ever be a fifth one' (I.15).[5] It is also important to note that the entire Sanskrit *kāvyaśāstra* tradition had seen *kāvya* as a systematic deviation or *vakratā* from the ordinary form of speech. In the first chapter of this study, we saw critics like Bhāmaha, Daṇḍin, Udbhaṭa, Ānandavardhana, Abhinavagupta, Mammaṭa and so on treating literature as a conscious departure from the quotidian use of language. This shows that the idea of *vakrokti* or deviant utterance was a central concern throughout Sanskrit literary tradition.

Kuntaka and *Svabhāvokti*

Although Bhāmaha laid out the basic framework of the idea of *vakrokti* and his successors like Daṇḍin, Rudraṭa and Ānandavardhana took it up in their poetic theory, none of them, in fact, treated the idea of *vakrokti* as a major concern of their critical inquiry. We find a detailed exposition of the idea of *vakrokti* only in *Vakroktijīvita* of the 10th-century Kashmiri critic, Kuntaka. *Vakroktijīvita*, as I have pointed out in the introduction of this study, came down to us in a somewhat fragmentary form without any commentary, and the text continues to remain incomplete without the last chapter. However, since all the major topics that Kuntaka promises to take up are covered in the first three chapters of *Vakroktijīvita*, we have all the reasons to think that nothing much of the text has been lost. His florid compositional style which is a clear departure from the usual way of employing Sanskrit in literary treatises seems to be an open endorsement of the critical position he details in his text.

According to Kuntaka, the very essence of *kāvya* is *vakrokti* or the art of presenting something in a fashion which is antithetical to the way we have experienced it so far. According to Kuntaka, the sound and sense in *kāvya* necessarily need to be adorned with the ornament called *vakrokti*. Kuntaka defines *vakrokti* as 'that signification which is different from the popular usage [*prasidhābhidhānavyatirekiṇī*]' (2009: 91). Kuntaka divides *vakrokti* into five broad categories such as *varṇa-vinyāsa-vakratā*, *pada-pūrvārtha-vakratā*, *pada-parārtha-vakratā*, *vākya-vakratā*, *prakaraṇa-vakratā* and *prabandha-vakratā*.[6] *Varṇa-vinyāsa-vakratā* is the skilful employment of syllables—especially consonants—in such a way that they appear strikingly different from their employment in the ordinary use of language (I.19). *Pada-pūrvārtha-vakratā* is the deviant utterance at the level of words (106).[7] *Pada-parārtha-vakratā* is the artistic deviation of the terminal part of words which decides the tense, number, gender, etc., of a signifier (II.26–34).[8] *Vākya-vakratā* is the figurative deviation at the sentence level (III.1–16). *Prakaraṇa-vakratā* is artistic deviation through episodes that make up a plot (588)[9] and *prabandha-vakratā* is the deviant utterance at the level of plot (651).[10]

According to Kuntaka, what makes a linguistic composition a *kāvya* or literary artefact is the presence of *alaṅkāra* (2009: 60), and the only *alaṅkāra* or ornament that can adorn a poem is *vakrokti.* What Kuntaka means by this statement is that *vakrokti* is the essence of all *alaṅkāra*s and there is no *alaṅkāra* without it. Kuntaka says:

> These two—sound and sense [which constitute a poem]—are *alaṅkāryās*, things that are to be decorated. They are to be embellished by some *alaṅkāra*s. What should function as the ornament of these two? . . . It is none other than deviant utterance [*vakrokti*]. *Vakrokti* is that signification which is different from the popular usage [*prasidhābhidhāna-vyatirekiṇī*] . . . This is what I am driving at—in *kāvya*, both sound and sense have separate existence. We are not adorning them with different *alaṅkāra*s. What serves as their ornament is their presentation in a deviant manner? Only this can cause beauty in poetry.[11] (91–92)

Considering figurative deviation (*vakratā*) as the vital component of *kāvya*, Kuntaka says that *svabhāvokti* or 'the presentation of an idea or entity in the way they are popularly presented or perceived in society' [*svabhāvasya padārthadharmalakṣaṇasya parispandasya uktirabhidhā*] (93) does not have any space within the ambit of *kāvya.* Kuntaka presents his opponent's view that *svabhāvokti* is an *alaṅkāra,* not to endorse it, but to systematically refute it:

> Here is an opponent's view: 'It has been stated by you [Kuntaka] that *vakrokti* is the only *alaṅkāra* and nothing other than *vakrokti* is an *alaṅkāra.* Why do you say so? The ancient *ālaṅkārikas* [literary theoreticians] had clearly stated that there is an *alaṅkāra* called *svabhāvokti*; this figure of speech is very charming.'
>
> To refute this observation, I [Kuntaka] say so: 'Those *ālaṅkārika*s, who say that *svabhāvokti* . . . is an *alaṅkāra,* are undoubtedly immature . . . What is *svabhāvokti?* It is the act of stating the nature of objects in the way they exist in the world. If that is an *alaṅkāra*, then what can be used to decorate it to become the body of *kāvya*?' (92–93)

We saw that *svabhāvokti* is the act of re-producing ideas and entities in the way they are dominantly perceived and presented in the world. The primary problem underpinning *svabhāvokti* is that it always goads the creative writer to verbatim re-produce an already existing familiar pattern of perception, thereby leaving little space for the author to be creative and original. To put it in the terminology of Deleuze and Guattari, *svabhāvokti* is 'decalcomaniac in nature'. A term borrowed from decorative technique, decalcomania is the superimposition of a predetermined pattern of engraving or print upon a new terrain. According to Deleuze and Guattari, decalcomania is static and 'uncreative' in the sense that it is a mere tracing of a primordial structure upon a new terrain (1983: 13). Just like a decalcomaniac tracing, *svabhāvokti* asks the creative writer to reproduce in *kāvya* a predetermined structure without any creative intervention. It never demands any originality or creativity on the part of the writer and always results in mere repetition and boredom.

Not only does *svabhāvokti* curb the creativity of the writer but it also imposes ontological certitude upon the entities that are being portrayed. Ontological certitude is the act of reducing the identity of an entity to a set of fixed assumptions that we have about it. We already saw that *svabhāvokti* is the reproduction of what is generally considered to be the 'essence', 'identity' or 'nature' of an entity. This shows that *svabhāvokti* always forces the creative writer to conform to the dominant conception of the identity of an entity. The idea of *svabhāva* always presupposes that an entity has an essence or identity inherent to it. This idea of *svabhāva* was central to some pre-Mahayana schools of Buddhism like *Sarvāstivāda*, which employs the term *svabhāva* to denote 'the permanent or unchanging substratum of an object' (Keown 2004: 286). According to them, *svabhāva* is an innate, inalienable 'mark' (*lakṣaṇā* or *svalakṣaṇā*) of entities. Summarising the pre-Mahayana conception of *svabhāva*, Christopher Bartley says,

> Each *dharma* [thing] has a fixed essence or intrinsic nature of its own (*svabhāva*). It is this possession of a permanent, fixed identity that differentiates the *dharmas* from the macroscopic aggregates. *Svabhāva* means intrinsic nature consisting in a specific inherent characteristic

> or power (*svalakṣaṇā*). The *svabhāva* of earth atoms is solidity, that of water atoms is fluidity and that of fire atoms heat. (2011: 27)

From this observation, it could be drawn that *svabhāvokti* or a statement which conforms to the dominant conception about the identity of an entity is an essentialist discourse. This view always aims to limit an entity's 'nature' or 'identity' to a set of fixed attributes. In other words, *svabhāvokti* reduces the essence of an entity to a fixed framework and functions as if the entity does not have any essence beyond that permanent framework.

As opposed to simply re-creating what is generally considered the identity of an entity (*svabhāva*), Kuntaka is concerned with the creative transformation of the existing structures and he never aims to reproduce the known and the familiar as it is generally perceived or represented. Kuntaka opines that the task of a poet is to portray the world differently through *vakratā* (deviation from what is familiar), as opposed to confining to the familiar equations of perception or *svabhāva*. He clarifies his stand further:

> This is the gist of what I have said—the objects that poets describe are not newly created on earth. Poets impart ordinary objects a sublime and non-ordinary form. They are elevated to such a rare position where they appeal to the hearts of the responsive readers. . . . Thus, poets transform ordinary entities into a non-ordinary and rare state. In this way, the objects that are described transcend the habitual way they have so far been perceived, and shine forth as if they are absolutely new entities, and ultimately steal our hearts. This is why poets are called 'creators.' As it is stated [by Ānandavardhana]: In the endless world of poetry, poet is the only lord. The whole world transforms at his will.[12] (2009: 342)

In Kuntaka's poetic theory, if a statement wants to attain the status of an *alaṅkāra* and consequently that of a *kāvya*, it should always be characterised by *vakratā*. While *svabhāvokti* is a habitual act of re-presenting an object in the same way it has been dominantly conceived and *vakrokti* is a 'creative' act that aims to transcend the habitual structures of perception.

Vakrokti and Creative Transformation

We have seen that *svabhāvokti* or the presentation of objects in the way they are dominantly perceived impedes a writer's creativity and imposes ontological certitude upon entities, whereas *vakrokti* parts ways with *svabhāvokti* by presenting ideas and entities distinctly different from what is generally thought to be their essence. In this section, I will explicate Kuntaka's resistance to the notion of *svabhāva* through the examples of vakrokti Kuntaka himself gives in *Vakroktijīvita*. For this, I explore representative examples from each of the five categories of *vakrokti* that Kuntaka mentions, namely, *varṇa-vinyāsa-vakratā*, *pada-pūrvārtha-vakratā*, *pada-parārtha-vakratā*, *vākya-vakratā*, *prakaraṇa-vakratā* and finally *prabandha-vakratā*. These five categories respectively deal with syllable (*varṇa*), word (*pada*), sentence (*vākya*), terminal parts of words determining the grammatical structure underpinning a sentence (*pada-parārtha*), and finally, the content or aesthetic emotion (*rasa*) of a literary work in total (*prakaraṇa* or *prabandha*).

The first example that I am going to deal with is *varṇa-vinyāsa-vakrata* wherein Sanskrit syllables are arranged in such a way that the 'familiar' way we use syllables in our daily life is transformed into a defamiliarised state. Kuntaka defines *varṇa-vinyāsa-vakratā* as the arrangement of the same consonants at short successive intervals in such a way that their arrangement *appears different from the usual way we arrange them in ordinary language* (*prasiddhaprasthānavyatirekiṇā*; 105). Kuntaka says,

> The point is that the deviant employment of syllables is at par with the deviant use of consonants, and it is of three kinds namely the successive repetition of one type of consonant, the successive repetition of two

consonants of the same category and the successive repetition of more than two consonants of the same category. (2009: 122)

The following is an example of *varṇa-vinyāsa-vakratā* that Kuntaka refers to:

prathamamaruṇacchāyāyastāvat-
tataḥ kanakaprabhas-
tadanu virahottāmyattanvī-
kapolatalataladyutiḥ |
prasarati tato dhvāntkṣoda-
kṣamaḥ kṣaṇadāmukhe
sarasabisinīkandaccheda
cchavirmṛgalāñchanaḥ || (214)
[Taking reddish glow in the beginning,
then the lustre of gold and then the colour on the cheek of a pining damsel,
and finally the glow of the root of lotus plants,
the sun rose up in the sky to remove darkness.]

In the verse quoted above, we have successive repetitions of consonants *ma* (in the first line), *ta* (in the second, third and fourth lines), *kṣa* (in the sixth line) and *cha* (in the seventh line). According to Kuntaka, *varṇa-vinyāsa-vakratā* is employed with the specific intention of using syllables distinctly different from the conventional way in which they are employed (*prasiddhaprasthānavyatirekiṇā*; 105). This arrangement of syllables in an unconventional fashion goes against our familiar and dominant equations of employing consonants in daily life. By arranging syllables in a deviant fashion, Kuntaka openly takes a detour from the conventional manner in which the syllables were dominantly used in ordinary speech, thus liberating the author and reader from the onus of repetition and habit. This conscious attempt to resist conformity can be observed at all the advanced stages of Kuntaka's engagement with language.

The second major category of *vakratā* is *pada-pūrvārtha-vakratā* or deviant utterance at the level of words. To see how *pada-pūrvārtha-vakratā* poses a resistance to the *svabhāva* of a word, let us have a look at *rūḍhī-vaicitrya-vakratā* which is one of the numerous varieties of *pada-pūrvārtha-vakratā* that Kuntaka refers to. We know that the relation between a signifier and its signified in any language is a matter of convention. Convention always imposes a definite *svabhāva* or ontology upon a signifier in the form of a specific signification. The *svabhāva* or the fixed semantic ontology conventionally attributed to a signifier functions as a limiting force upon a signifier by assigning that signifier a specific meaning or set of meanings. It is this static *svabhāva* with which we often identify a word that gets challenged in Kuntaka's *rūḍhī-vaicitrya-vakratā*. In *rūḍhī-vaicitrya-vakratā*, a word leaves its conventional meaning and comes to suggest a new meaning. Kuntaka opines, 'When words are seen to denote meanings that are not conventionally associated with it, we get what is called "art in beautifying conventional sense"' [*rūḍhī-vaicitrya-vakratā*] (231). The following is an example of *rūḍhī-vaicitrya-vakratā* that Kuntaka cites from Ānandavardhana's *Dhvanyāloka*.

> Virtues bloom,
> when appreciated by connoisseurs of art.
> When blessed by the rays of the sun,
> a lotus becomes a lotus.[13] (233)

In this verse, the term 'lotus' undergoes an ontological change, when it occurs for the second time. The literal meaning of the word 'lotus' is that it is 'a tropical plant with white or pink flowers growing on the surface of lakes'. If we take the word 'lotus' in its literal sense, when it occurs a second time in the given context, the whole sentence will not make any sense. Therefore, the term 'lotus' in its second occurrence undergoes an incorporeal transformation. That is to say, although the word's physicality does not change, its identity or *svabhāva* in terms of its meaning undergoes a drastic change. In its second occurrence, the word 'lotus' no longer signifies its literal meaning—a tropical flower. On the other hand, it attains a new meaning—'perfection'. So, it means that a lotus attains a state of perfection, only when it is blessed by the rays of the sun. Thus, the word 'lotus' leaves its *svabhāva* and attains a new linguistic identity. This incorporeal transformation functions as a new aesthetic experience for both the author and the reader who are otherwise forced to conceive the word 'lotus' in a more or less static manner.

The third category that Kuntaka deals with is *vākya-vakratā* which is deviant utterance at the level of a *vākya* or sentence. To put it in Kuntaka's words,

> A sentence means a group of words. It contains indeclinable words, cases, adjectives, verbs and its different forms. It [*vākya-vakratā*] is the deviant utterance of sentences like a *śloka*. It is the deviant utterance of speech in a sentence. That is, this variety of deviant utterance depends on the deviant use of a group of words. (127)

As far as Kuntaka is considered, the whole conventional category of *alaṅkāra* is subsumed in this category. Kuntaka in the first chapter of *Vakroktijīvita* observes, 'The whole section of *alaṅkāra* will fall within this category' (217). Therefore, let us examine how Kuntaka's idea of *vākya-vakratā* functions as a transformative and creative act through an exploration of certain select categories of figures of speech.

What I cite here as the first instance of *vākya-vakratā* is the figure of speech called *aprastuta-praśaṃsa*. The literal meaning of *aprastuta-praśaṃsa* is 'praise by means of the extraneous'. In *aprastuta-praśaṃsa*, the *prastuta* or 'the matter at hand' is praised through a statement about something extraneous. In *Vakroktijīvita*, Kuntaka says, '*Aprastuta-praśaṃsa* is that sort of *alaṅkāra* where an apparently dissimilar idea is connected with the matter at hand in order to enhance the beauty of the latter' (2009: III.192). The following is an example of *aprastuta-praśaṃsa* that Kuntaka mentions in *Vakroktijīvita*:

> What a charming river is this,
> where water lilies float over with the moon!
> From this unique river of allurement there also emerge the cranial lobes of an elephant, the trunks of plantain trees, and the fibrous stems of lotus plants! (456)

This verse which Kuntaka has taken from Vikramāditya's *Sūktimuktāvali* portrays how a certain damsel appears to a young man. In this verse, the speaker is not simply reproducing the image of a lady in the way she is usually perceived. Rather, he moves away from the general perception (*svabhāva*) about a woman's body parts and sees them in a new light. In the given verse, the body of the damsel in its entirety is presented as a 'river', her sidelong glances as 'water lilies', her face as 'the moon', her breasts as 'the cranial lobes of an elephant', her thighs as 'trunks of plantain trees' and her arms as 'lotus stems'. Abhinavagupta in his commentary on this passage in *Dhvanyāloka* says:

> This is the speech of a certain young man . . . In it the word 'river' suggests the fullness [of a lady's beauty], the word 'water lilies,' the sidelong glances of her eyes, 'the moon,' her face, the words 'elephant's cranial lobes,' her breasts, 'trunks of plantain trees,' her thighs, and 'lotus stems,' her arms. (1990: 597–598)[14]

This verse that Kuntaka cites as the example of *vākya-vakratā* is a 'creative' act wherein the speaker imposes a set of new images upon the body parts of a lady, as opposed to merely talking about them in an ordinary fashion.

The *pada-parārtha-vakratā* deals with the grammatical structure governing a sentence. Before we analyse how *vakrokti* functions vis-à-vis grammar, it is important to problematise the very idea of grammar itself. Grammar, as we all know, is a set of structural rules concerning the composition of words and sentences in any language. In any linguistic system, grammar structures language in a specific fashion and forces the users of language to abide by the structures it prescribes.

In other words, it imposes a specific ontology or *svabhāva* upon the way we use language in general. Umberto Eco notes, 'The given language obliges me to choose between masculine and feminine, and forbids me to conceive a neuter category; it obliges me to engage the other by either "thou" or "you"; I have no right to leave my affective and social relationship unspecified' (1995: 240–241). This shows that grammar is a discourse controlling the very nature of any language. Barthes says that language imposes a kind of servility upon its users by forcing them to use the language in a specific fashion. According to Barthes, 'In speech, then, servility and power are inescapably intermingled' (1977: 6).

Kuntaka's theory of *vakrokti* aims to escape the rigid grammatical structures which subjugate us to follow a predetermined plan of action while using a language. As opposed to blindly re-presenting the existing structures of grammar, Kuntaka attempts to creatively intervene in the employment of grammatical structures. An analysis of an instance of *pada-parārtha-vakratā* which deals with the terminal part of a signifier will prove this point. For example, *saṃkhyā-vakratā* under the category of *pada-parārtha-vakratā* subverts the grammatical rules concerning the category of numbers in Sanskrit. Kuntaka says,

> The poets, who are very particular about making their composition poetically different, transpose numbers. Then we have what is known as *saṃkhyā-vakratā*. This is the purport of the sentence: wherever we need singular or plural form, another number is used, or different numbers are used in the same case relation, for the sake of poetic charm. (2009: 314)

In other words, if the conventional grammatical rule demands the use of a singular form, the poet would use either a dual or plural form. If a plural form is necessary, the poet would choose either a dual form or a singular form. The following is a case in point.

> Her eyes [*nayane*] are huge thickets [*kānanāni*] of full-bloomed *kūvala* blossoms and ponds of water-lilies [*sarojākarāḥ*] make her hands [*pāṇī*]. (315)

The term *nayane* in the given context is grammatically a dual form (two eyes). Here the lady's 'two eyes' (*nayane*) are compared to huge thickets (*kānana*). According to the grammatical conventions governing the number in Sanskrit, the word signifying 'eye' being the dual form, the 'thickets' (to which the 'eyes' are compared) should also be dual. That is to say, the poet should ideally use the dual form of the word *kānana* (which is *kānane*). But the author, in this specific context, uses the plural form of the word *kānana*, that is, *kānanāni*, thus consciously flouting the rules of grammar in Sanskrit. Similarly, in the second line, *pāṇī* (two hands) is grammatically a dual form. Two hands (*pāṇi*) being compared to the 'ponds of water-lilies', the number of ponds should also be dual, that is, *sarojanākare*. But, in the given verse, this grammatical rule is not followed; instead, the plural form *sarojākarāḥ* is employed in place of the dual *sarojanākare*.

An analysis of *puruṣa-vakratā*—another category in *pada-parārtha vakratā*—will further prove this point. Kuntaka says, 'When in poetry, the first person and the other persons are interchangeably used so as to achieve artistic excellence, we have deviant use of persons (*puruṣa-vakratā*)' (2009: 316). As an example of *puruṣa-vakratā*, Kuntaka quotes the following verse from *Tāpasavatsarāja* which depicts the minister Gaudanārāyaṇa's advice to Vāsavadattā:

> I know that our Kauśāmbi is conquered by enemies
> and our undiplomatic king is weak.
> Women's hearts always pain at the parting of their dear ones—
> I don't mean to talk about it now.
> Now, devi *you* may please know what you need to do next
> (*jānātu devi svayam*). (317)

According to Sanskrit grammar, the subject of the last sentence is 'you' which is *madhyamā-puruṣa ekavacana* (second person, singular). The *dhāturūpa* (the base form) of the verb used here is *jñā* which means 'to know'. And the tense that is employed here is *lot lakār* (present imperative tense). If we go by the rules of Sanskrit grammar, when the subject is second person singular in *lot lakār*, the sentence should be—*jānīhī devī svayam*. But in the given example, the poet consciously subverts this rule and says *jānātu devī svayam*. Here the grammatical rule underlying *lot lakār-prathama puruṣa-ekavacana* (present imperative tense, first person singular) is used, instead of *lot lakār-madhyamā puruṣa-ekavacana* (present imperative tense, second person singular).

Vakrokti is not limited to the aforementioned linguistic categories. It is also concerned with the deviant representation of emotion and content as we find it in *prakaraṇa-vakratā* and *prabandha-vakratā*. While *prakaraṇa-vakratā* deals with content or emotion at the episodic level, *prabandha-vakratā* deals with them at the plot level. Since both these varieties deal with the same subject matter, here, I representatively use only *prabandha-vakratā* to prove my point. A glance at one of the *prabandha-vakratā*s will show us how Kuntaka transforms the familiar emotion and content of a familiar story in a defamiliarised fashion. According to Kuntaka, 'When there is a departure from the *rasa* of the source book, and a new *rasa* is delineated [in the same story] by the poet so as to delight the heart of the readers, we should regard it as "artistic deviance at the plot level" (*prabandha-vakratā*)' (2009: 651). The example that Kuntaka cites for this category of *vakratā* is Bhavabhūti's *Uttararāmacarita* which is based on Vālmīki's *Rāmāyaṇa*. The conventional plot of the *Rāmāyaṇa* ends in *karuṇa rasa* (tragic emotion) with Sītā vanishing into the earth and Rāma walking into the river Sarayū. But in *Uttararāmacarita*, this story is transformed in such a way that the readers experience *śṛṅgāra rasa* (erotic emotion) instead of *karuṇa rasa*. Kuntaka observes,

> Here is *Uttararāmacarita*, another example. In the *Rāmāyaṇa*, Sītā who had undergone extreme pang of separation goes down into the netherworld. Raghupati, along with his brother, walks into the river. Thus, the *kāvya* ends in *karuṇa rasa*. But in the drama *Uttararāmacarita*, the story is completely changed. The courage of

> Lava and Kuśa becomes a feast for the spectators' eyes. The union (*saṃbhoga-śṛṅgāra*) of Rāma and Sītā, at the end of the drama, becomes a matter of joy for the noble audience and it adds to the beauty of the drama. We can find a lot of other examples of this ilk. (653)

Another similar example that Kuntaka cites is *Veṇīsaṃhāra* of Bhaṭṭa Nārāyaṇa which is based on the *Mahābhārata*. The *aṅgi rasa* or the overall emotion of the *Mahābhārata* is *śānta rasa*. But in *Veṇīsaṃhāra*, the author changes the *aṅgi rasa* of the story from the dominant *śānta rasa* to *vīra rasa*. Kuntaka says,

> The *Mahabharata* being an epic which portrays the futility of earthly instincts based on numerous desires devouring wisdom and emotion, *śānta rasa* is its ultimate emotion. But the dramatist leaves aside *śānta rasa* and incorporates *vīra rasa* which suits the story of the Pāṇḍavas. The story ends with the glorious emergence of Dharmaputra, who in spite of losing his army, reaches the zenith of royal esteem. Because of this beauty of *vakratā* which pervades the entire work, the noble readers achieve delight from the drama. They get energized, seeing the Pāṇḍavas conquering their enemies with their sheer courage and then enjoying prosperity. (652)

In these examples, the author is not simply replicating the already existing emotion of the story. On the other hand, he changes the pre-given story into a new product so that the readers enjoy a new experience. Kuntaka's observation about this restructuring of a familiar plot is particularly notable here. Kuntaka says that when *vakrokti* is properly used, even literary works which deal with the same story look different, just as different creatures of the same species do not look alike (666).

These examples that we have seen in this chapter show that the idea of *vakrokti* theorised by Kuntaka is concerned with the creative transformation of the existing structures. Kuntaka never aims to reproduce the known and the familiar. While the rigid structures of *svabhāva* always prevent 'experimentation' with the existing pattern, *vakrokti* is always an experimentation with the existing structures.

Krishnamoorthy's observation about Kuntaka's concept of *vakrokti* merits attention here. He says,

> His [Kuntaka's] *vakrokti* is an inevitable and deliberate departure from the empirical linguistic mode to achieve aesthetic effect. It is a deviation from common parlance dictated by the very necessities of poetic facts and it is not an intellectual but imaginative activity. These basic postulates of Kuntaka can find echoes in modern aesthetic theories. (1977: xxxix)

The term 'experimentation' coined by Deleuze and Guattari, is very much tenable in our discussion of *vakrokti.* According to Deleuze and Guattari, experimentation is a resistance to all the known and experienced patterns. Experimentation always aims to go beyond the available structures of perception and performance. It is always an open-ended process which explores the possibilities of newer experiences, as opposed to reproducing something already experienced and familiar. The process of experimentation is inseparable from innovation and it always aims to dismantle the old combinations in order to generate entities that are so far non-existent (Deleuze and Guattari 1983: 371). Kuntaka's theory of *vakrokti* which aims to transcend the boundaries of the familiar and the experienced is undoubtedly a process of experimentation. Such a process works towards the goal of creative transformation and helps entities come out of the onus of the ontological certitude that we have imposed upon them. It is also a liberating experience for poets and readers of *kāvya* as it provides them with a platform to rupture their familiar equations of performance and perception.

Vakrokti and *Atiśaya*

Having explained how the idea of *vakrokti* turns out to be a liberating experience for the author as well as the objects that are portrayed, we can now examine the concept of *vakrokti* vis-à-vis the experience of the reader. What a reader elicits from his/her encounter with the defamiliarised form of a familiar object is undoubtedly the feeling of *atiśaya* or surprise. In *vakrokti*, a reader experiences the feeling of surprise or *atiśaya*, when s/he witnesses the hitherto unseen facet of a familiar object or idea. A speech that creates surprise in the readers through the defamiliarised representation of entities and ideas is called *atiśayokti*. For Bhāmaha, *atiśayokti* is synonymous with *vakrokti* (49). In his commentary on Ānandavardhana's citation of Bhāmaha's observations about *vakrokti* and *atiśayokti*, Abhinavagupta holds that *atiśayokti* and *vakrokti* are the same, and they constitute the very soul of all figures of speech. Abhinava says,

> That which has been defined as hyperbole is the whole of figured speech, that is, is every sort of figure of speech, for Bhāmaha has said: An unusual or striking form of word or meaning (*vakrokti)* is considered an ornament (*alaṅkṛti*) of poetic utterance. For the 'bent' (*vakra*) form of a word or of a meaning (*ukti*) is its presentation in an unusual or striking form (*lokottirnena rapena)* and this constitutes the ornament of a figure of speech (*alaṅkārasyālaṅkaraḥ*). Now hyperbole is precisely the property of being unusual or striking (*lokottarata*). Hence hyperbole is a common property of all figures of speech. Thus . . . it is by this hyperbole that a meaning which has been worn out by everyone's use of it can be given new variety and interest. (1990: 264)

In *Vakroktijīvita*, Kuntaka also repeats the same observation. For him, *atiśayokti* which is the very life force of all ornaments of *kāvya* (*sarvālaṅkāra-jīvitaṃ*) is present in all sorts of *vakratā*s (477–478). The term *atiśayokti* in this context should not be understood in its limited sense as an individual *alaṅkāra* but in its broader sense as an experience utterance generating an experience of surprise. The term *atiśayokti* in Sanskrit is composed of two words—*atiśaya* and *ukti*, meaning respectively 'surprise' and 'speech'. So the term *atiśayokti*, in its etymological sense, means any linguistic expression which causes surprise in the reader or spectator.

A glance at a few definitions of the term *atiśayokti* will help us better understand this observation. Bhāmaha says, 'Where something, transcending ordinary experience, is described without reason, it is regarded as the figure *atiśayokti*' (1998: II.52). According to Daṇḍin, *atiśayokti* 'is that great *alaṅkāra* where signification (*vivakṣā*) moves beyond the borders of common perception (*lokasīmātivarttinī*)' (1962: II.214). According to Udbhaṭa, 'A statement, with a cause, transcending the common perception of people—the learned consider it to be the *alaṅkāra atiśayokti*' (1982: 79). Udbhaṭa divides *atiśayokti* into four varieties—'imposition of sameness where there is a difference in reality', 'imagining difference where there is really no difference', 'describing some imaginary thing which is really impossible' and 'the reversion of cause and effect to show quickness of effect' (79). In all these varieties of *atiśayokti*, the ultimate aim is to shatter the reader's common perception of an entity.

From these observations, it may be drawn that *vakratā* is the means and *atiśaya* or surprise is the result of its employment. *Vakratā* always aims to re-sensitise the reader's experience with a familiar object by presenting it in a defamiliarised form. We know that a person's repeated exposure to a particular form of experience or the performance of a habitual act always results in 'desensitization' or diminished emotional response. Viktor Shklovsky's observation in his seminal essay 'Art as Technique' is noteworthy in this context. Shklovsky says that repeated exposure to an event or a pattern of experience generates automaticity, and consequently, a sense of predictability, in the perceiver, thereby reducing the element of surprise to the minimum. Shklovsky observes:

> If we start to examine the general laws of perception, we see that as perception becomes habitual, it becomes automatic. Thus, for example, all of our habits retreat into the area of the unconsciously automatic; if one remembers the sensations of holding a pen or of speaking in a foreign language for the first time and compares that with his feeling at performing the action for the ten thousandth time, he will agree

> with us. Such habituation explains the principles by which, in ordinary speech, we leave phrases unfinished and words half expressed. In this process, ideally realized in algebra, things are replaced by symbols. Complete words are not expressed in rapid speech; their initial sounds are barely perceived. Alexander Pogodin offers the example of a boy considering the sentence 'The Swiss mountains are beautiful' in the form of a series of letters: T, S, m, a, b. (1965: 11)

In a *vakrokti kāvya*, readers are pushed out of their comfort zone of predictability and attain a new perception of the already existing structures.

There is also a possibility that this process of presenting a familiar structure in a defamiliarised form can also shock the readers, as opposed to surprising them. Hans Robert Jauss's 'horizon of expectation' speaks of this bipolar nature of deviation from the established order. Jauss holds that every generation of readers will possess a 'horizon of expectation' or a shared mental state of a particular generation to understand, evaluate and interpret a text or an artwork (1982: 23). As long as the pattern of the new text conforms to the readers' 'horizon of expectation', there are no problems. But if there is a deviation from 'the horizon of expectation', it can affect the reader in two ways—either the text can please and surprise the reader through its unconventionality, or it can shock the readers, making them resistant to the new deviant approach (25). In the theoretical position of *vakrokti*, Kuntaka's attempt—in spite of his avowed plan of effecting a change in the reader's 'horizon of expectation'—is to give the readers a pleasant experience. According to Kuntaka, although deviant utterance is an essential component of *kāvya*, it should be pleasing to the reader (*tadvidāhlādakāriṇi*) (2009: 61) by keeping the deviation within the larger framework of the existing moral and social values.

Discordance with the existing moral and social value systems of the reader is often an important reason for a deviant utterance turning into an unpleasant experience. Therefore Kuntaka, like his predecessors such as Bhāmaha, Daṇḍin and Ānandavardhana, is extremely mindful of the social decorum of the period. Keeping in mind the fact that impropriety can cause the readers to have discomfiture, Kuntaka asks the creative writers to employ deviant utterance in such a way that it does not challenge the dominant value system or propriety of the reader. Kuntaka says: 'For the spoiling of *rasa*, there is no cause other than impropriety' (*anaucityādṛte nānyadrasabhaṅgasya kāraṇam*; 2009: 404). An example of a deviant utterance turning into a shocking experience would be the representation of a putative noble character as a degenerate figure, wanting in prowess and moral integrity. Citing the reason that the representation of an event which is at war with the readers' value system can cause the readers to have discomfort, Kuntaka instructs the poets to rewrite situations which do not conform to the social propriety of the time. In the previous chapter, we saw Kuntaka's comment on the scene where Rāma goes to hunt the golden deer. In the *Rāmāyaṇa*, upon hearing the cry of Rāma who went to catch the golden deer, his brother Lakṣmaṇa goes in search of him. But in the drama *Udāttarāghava*, this plot is rewritten in such a way that it is Rāma who goes to rescue Lakṣmaṇa, not the other way around. This change is deliberately made in the play so that the play conforms to the social propriety of the period which says that it is highly improper for a man of great prowess and courage like Rāma to be rescued by his younger brother Lakṣmaṇa (2009: I.21).

This shows that notwithstanding his attempts to resist the ontological certitude imposed upon entities through deviant utterance, Kuntaka neither becomes critical of the social decorum of his society nor jars the readers out of the comfort zone of their value system. As far as Kuntaka is concerned, the aim of *kāvya* is to impart pleasure to the reader. Hence, even when he attempts to challenge the dominantly conceived *svabhāva* of entities, Kuntaka makes sure that the change in 'the horizon of expectation' does not create a dissonance in the psyche of readers.

In this chapter, we saw that Kuntaka's theory of *vakrokti* poses a strong resistance to the habitual frameworks of performance and perception, and sees literature as a transformative act which presents familiar objects in a defamiliarised fashion. This act of defamiliarisation in the first instance is a liberating experience for the author in the sense that it provides the author with an opportunity to transcend the familiar equations of perception and performance. In this process, it also releases the entity (which is being portrayed) from our rigid conventional conception of it. Equally liberating is the experience of the reader who encounters this deviant representation. Through their encounter with the hitherto unseen facet of a familiar object, readers broaden the horizon of their perception, and experience what is called *atiśaya* or surprise. It is also significant to note that in spite of Kuntaka's insistence on the employment of *vakratā* in *kāvya*, he opines that a creative writer should not attempt to shock the readers by employing deviant utterance in such a way that it breaks the norms of propriety in society. *Vakrokti*, for Kuntaka, is always subordinated to the idea of social propriety and the feeling of surprise and pleasure.

5

Towards an Interventionist Intellectual Historiography

Not fare well,
But fare forward voyagers.
—T.S. Eliot, 'The Dry Salvages'

What ensures the live continuum of any epistemology—be it ancient or modern—is a strong, critical engagement with it. It not only prevents an intellectual tradition from becoming ossified in nature but also keeps the tradition alive and contemporary. As far as the Indian *kāvyaśāstra* (poetics) tradition is concerned, attempts to step beyond the existing truth claims were its very life force. In many texts in Sanskrit literary criticism, one can clearly observe what is traditionally known as the *pūrvapakṣa* strategy (wherein an author explains the views of their predecessor or contemporary to refute them systematically) to register their dissent with the existing truth claims. For instance, the theories of *guṇa* (the theory of poetic merit) and *rīti* (the theory of poetic style) were the offshoots of dissent with the views of *ālaṅkārika*s (the literary critics who believe that the ornamentation of speech is the soul of poetry). *Dhvani* (theory of poetic suggestion) was the result of dissent with the views of the exponents of *guṇa* and *rīti*, and the *anumāna* (the theory of inference) school had considerable differences of opinion with the exponents of the *dhvani* school.

Even a cursory glance at a few debates regarding the nature of *rasa*, recorded by Abhinavagupta in his commentary on Ānandavardhana's *Dhvanyāloka*, will further show us that the spirit of dissent and debate was the very hallmark of the intellectual tradition of Sanskrit *kāvyaśāstra*. Bhaṭṭa Lollaṭa is the first commentator of Bharata's *Nāṭyaśāstra* to take up this debate regarding the ontology of *rasa*. According to Lollaṭa, *rasa* is nothing but stable emotions strengthened (*upacita*) by *vibhāva*, *anubhāva* and *vyabhicāribhāva*. For him, *rasa* is actually located in the character (*anukārya*), although we can figuratively say that the actor also contains *rasa* by the power of his identification (*anusādhana*) with the character. But Lollaṭa's successor Śaṃkuka repudiates this view by arguing that *rasa* is not the augmentation of stable emotions in the character. According to Śaṃkuka, *rasa* is not produced either in the actor or in the character but is inferred by the spectator from the aesthetic elements employed by the actor on stage. Śaṃkuka's successor Bhaṭṭa Nāyaka has a different opinion on this matter. Bhaṭṭa Nāyaka opines that *rasa* is not inferred by the spectators. On the other hand, spectators experience *rasa* through a special function called *bhāvana*. Other than these views we have seen, Abhinavagupta further identifies various other opinions about the nature of *rasa*. Abhinava observes:

> Still others say that *rasa* is the *vibhava* alone, others that it is the *anubhava* alone, and some that it is the *sthayibhava* alone, some that it is the *vyabhicaribhava,* still others that the combination of these four is *rasa*. Some say that *rasa* is the character being portrayed. Others say that *rasa* is the conglomeration of these five elements. (1992: 223–224)

This strong sense of critical thinking continued to exist in *kāvyaśāstra* even in the medieval period, which is often wrongly dubbed as the dark age of India's past by imperialist historiographers. To mark their intellectual departure from their predecessors, as Yigal Bronner points out in his article 'What is New and What is Navya: Sanskrit Poetics on the Eve of Colonialism', Sanskrit literary theoreticians in the medieval phase often called themselves *navya*s or 'neo-intellectuals'. Jagannātha, Appayya Dīkṣita and Siddicandra are the three major critics from the medieval phase who embodied the spirit of debate and dissent in Sanskrit poetics. For example, Dīkṣhita's *Citramīmāṃsā* (*The Investigation of the Colourful*) redefined the views of the *prācīnas* (ancients), such as Mammaṭa, Vidyānātha, Bhoja and Ruyyaka. Similarly, Jagannātha's *Citramīmāṃsa-khaṇḍana* (*The Refutation of the Investigation of the Colourful*), another seminal text in Sanskrit poetics from the medieval phase, challenged many views endorsed by his predecessor Dīkṣita in his *Citramīmāṃsā*. Siddicandra's *Kāvyaprakāśa-khaṇḍana* (*The Refutation of the Light on Poetry*) is self-evidently a criticism of Mammaṭa's *Kāvyaprakāśa* (*The Light on Poetry*), which had, by then, achieved the colossal status of a rulebook with numerous commentaries on it from different parts of the Sanskrit cosmopolis. But this tradition of debate and dissent, which was the very soul of Sanskrit poetics, started disappearing from the scene during the colonial period. It is this decline that Pollock underlines:

> The two centuries before European colonialism decisively established itself in the subcontinent around 1750 constitute one of the most innovative epochs of Sanskrit systematic thought (in language analysis, logic, hermeneutics, moral, legal philosophy, and the rest). Thinkers produced new formulations of old problems, in entirely new discursive idioms, in what were often new scholarly genres employing often a new historicist framework; some even called themselves . . . 'the new' scholars (*navya*). Concurrently with the spread of European power, however, this dynamism diminished so much that by 1800, the capacity of Sanskrit thought to make history had vanished. The production of moral-legal texts, for example, which was so extensive throughout the seventeenth-century, ceased entirely, and in core disciplines like hermeneutics or literary theory no significant scholarship—that is, significant in the eyes of the tradition itself—was again to be written. (2000: 1)

What triggered the sudden plummet of Sanskrit *kāvyaśāstra* from its apotheosis to a state of mere nominal existence was obviously the policies of the colonial government. The most prominent among them was undoubtedly the educational charter of 1813. The charter announced that

> [A] sum of not less than one lac rupees in each year shall be set apart and applied for the revival and improvement of literature, and the encouragement of learned natives of India, and for the introduction and promotion of a knowledge of the sciences among the inhabitants of the British territories in India. (Macaulay 2015: 43)

Following this charter, there emerged a heated debate regarding the medium and the mode of education that should be implemented in the educational institutions in colonial India. While a group of intellectuals called the Orientalists favoured the policy of encouraging Oriental literature in classical languages such as Sanskrit, Arabic and Persian, another sect known as Anglicists stood for the promotion of Western education. Finally, the disputes of both parties were submitted to Thomas Babington Macaulay who in 1835 recommended that Western education should be promoted in India through the medium of English.

In spite of the upper hand of the Anglicists in academia, the efforts of the Orientalists to keep up interest in the classical knowledge system undoubtedly bore fruit. Particularly important among their initiatives is the establishment of the Calcutta Madrassa by Warren Hastings (1781), the Benares Sanskrit College by Jonathan Duncan (1784) and the Asiatic Society of Bengal by William Jones (1791). This does not imply that the actions of the Orientalists to promote the classical epistemologies in India were unmotivated. Thapar observes, 'Much of this activity was fostered by the belief that knowledge about the colony would enable a greater control over it and would provide a firm foundation to the power that the colonial authorities exercised. This was thought to be "the necessary furniture of empire" . . .' (2002: 3). The aim behind the establishment of the Fort William College at Calcutta in 1800 was specifically to teach British officials the local language and tradition. In concurrence with this tendency, many texts of Sanskrit literary science, which were thought to be lost once and for all, were reconstructed from their available fragments. Many texts in Sanskrit poetics were translated into English and other vernacular languages. Scholars also spent a considerable amount of time and effort to reconstruct many *kāvyaśāstra* texts that were thought to be lost forever.

That said, one should note that the reason for this act was not the Empire's love for Indian knowledge systems. The representation of a glorious Sanskrit past as the apotheosis of culture in Indian history was an effective ideological tool for the empire's civilising mission. By presenting Sanskrit literature and other scholarly disciplines from what they called the Hindu period (ranging from the origins to 1300 CE) as the markers of a glorious period, Orientalist historiographers indoctrinated the idea that early India marked the heyday of Indian civilisation, and what followed—the medieval Muslim period—was a period of decadence and stagnation without any remarkable high points of cultural achievement.[1] According to Devy, 'the attitude of history implicit in Indological works ranging from Halhed's *Grammar of Bengali* (1780) to Max Müller's *India: What Can It Teach Us?* (1882), considers the Indian heritage as once glorious but now decadent force' (2009: 32).

The conception of a 'glorious' past instilled in the native scholars of Orientalist lineage an absolutely uncritical reverence towards the intellectual traditions from early India such as Sanskrit *kāvyaśāstra*. It prevented the native scholars from questioning all that is ancient to the point of treating it as holy and sacrosanct. This is one of the primary reasons why engagement with Sanskrit literary theories—as in the case of many other intellectual traditions from early India—got reduced to mere reproduction and restatement of the already available scholarship. In short, the colonial period witnessed the death of Sanskrit poetics as a live intellectual tradition by encouraging the native scholars to adopt a reverential attitude towards it. Rajeswari Sunder Rajan notes that 'the Orientalist task of revival [also] required the entire suppression of the hundred years of Muslim rule' (1986: 27) and the suppression of the knowledge systems produced during this period. During the postcolonial phase, especially in the 1980s, another attitudinal shift happened in studies on Sanskrit *kāvyaśāstra*. This shift which can be labelled a revivalist trend aimed to use Sanskrit poetics—either in its original form or with necessary modifications—as an effective tool to evaluate the literary merit of any modern Indian literary texts. This trend, which was spearheaded by Indian literary theoreticians such as K. Krishnamoorthy, Krishna Rayan, C.D. Narasimhaiah and so on was the result of a strong desire to decolonise our Western critical sensibilities and introduce an extreme nationalist trend in literary studies. Ashcroft and Tiffin talk about this revivalist disposition in their *The Empire Writes Back*:

> The main drive in re-employing terms from Sanskrit criticism, such as those listed above [rasa and dhvani], or from ancient Tamil (Ramanujan 1985) has been in assessing the literature produced in Indian vernacular languages where a direct continuity of some essential 'indianness' has been more vigorously asserted. Critics such as K. Krishnamoorthy (1984) claim the existence of a theoretical base common to all Indian literatures, including both post-Sanskrit and non-Sanskrit, a base that is itself the sign of an Indian sensibility. The Kannada-speaking novelist and critic U.R. Anantha Murthy presents a more complex view of the relation between contemporary vernacular texts and the Tamil and Sanskrit canon, a view which takes into account the literatures in 'english' as well as those in Indian languages. He suggests that the relationship of the ancient languages (Tamil and Sanskrit) to the modern vernaculars is analogous to that of Latin and modern English (Anantha Murthy 1986). The Kannada terms *marga/desi*; the *way* and the *earth* are, he claims, potent metaphors for this with Sanskrit as the way (*marga*) and the vernacular (e.g. Kannada) as the earth or ground (*desi*). All texts written in the present mix the two, just as all English texts demonstrate a varying mix of Latinate and vernacular elements (more redolent of the former in the case of, say, Milton, or of the latter in the case of, say, Keats). (2002: 117)

Although these critics aimed to decolonise themselves from the clutches of Western critical concepts, their attempt to vindicate the efficacy of Indian poetics remained mostly dependent on their

Western counterparts. To substantiate their claim that ancient Indian literary theories are 'modern' and sophisticated just like any other modern critical theory and have the potential to function as an analytical apparatus for contemporary literary texts, these critics compared Sanskrit *kāvyaśāstra* theories in their canonical form to their Western counterparts, especially the Formalist theoretical positions, and brought out the points of convergence shared by these two.[2] This comparativist approach was primarily a nativist answer to the Anglicist view about the Indian intellectual tradition 'that a single shelf of a good European library was worth the whole native literature of India and Arabia' (Macaulay 2015: 240). By comparing Sanskrit *kāvyaśāstra* theories in their canonical form to Western formalist literary positions, the exponents of the comparativist approach attempt to show that the corpus of knowledge from India's glorious past is modern and relevant in all spacio-temporal locations. Chandran's observation merits attention here. She opines that

> If this trace of Orientalism is disturbing to an Indian reader, what is more upsetting is the desire of much of Indian critical writing on Sanskrit aesthetics to validate it using western critical precepts. So Abhinavagupta is compared to Benedetto Croce or Susanne Langer in an effort to prove how prescient the ancient Indian philosopher-critic was. Indians who write about our classical literary theorists seem to 'protest too much' to demonstrate how 'we Indians had known it all so long ago'. Assertions like 'Bharata is indeed the Aristotle of India' or a comparison of Kalidasa with William Shakespeare betray our insecurity and lack of confidence. (2013: 28)

By showing that our ideas are similar to the modern Western critical positions, the advocates of the comparativist approach attempt to prove that Sanskrit literary theories are as 'valid' and 'advanced' as Western literary theories.[3]

Though this movement was initially lauded as reassuring and promising by many nativists, it was soon proven that it failed to yield the desired effect. Adopting a xenophobic approach towards the West, it aimed to bodily reproduce and apply the old critical sensibilities in the new world. In other words, this move was shorn of the sense of debate and criticism that Sanskrit *kāvyaśāstra* originally had, and Sanskrit poetics in the new system had only a vegetative existence. It brought this episteme to a teleological closure and prevented the production of any new knowledge about/from this knowledge system.

What is now undoubtedly needed is a critical engagement with these theoretical positions through debate, questioning and re-reading so that the generation of new systems of knowledge about these theoretical positions is possible. Only such an approach can ensure the continuum of this knowledge system. Keeping in line with this spirit, the prominent Malayalam critic, V.C. Sreejan says,

> Suppose, somebody generates a new thought from the ideas of Barthes, either by deconstructing them or by connecting them with other ideas. I call such a move an original and unique contribution. What matters is not where the knowledge comes from, but whether a new system of knowledge is produced. What I mean is that instead of considering our ancient epistemologies as the ultimate truth, we need to see them only as the beginning of the endless reconsiderations and deconstructions that are to come in future. (1999: 14–15; my translation)

What Sreejan calls for is an incessant re-reading of these bodies of knowledge. Only such an approach can open up a text to multiple possibilities of reading.

Although it is important to record how 'classical' knowledge systems were originally understood and practised, an obsession with this process in the realm of research will only impede new courses of development in this field. We must understand that any attempt to confer the title classic on a knowledge system will definitely foreclose its further development since a system of knowledge that claims to be classical always retains a rigid discursive boundary to uphold its value. It is surprising to note that 'the aesthetic or ethical quality of the product is not necessarily a function of the degree of creative freedom' exercised by the practitioner; on the contrary, 'the stricter and more rigorous the adherence to discipline, the more valued may be the outcome' (Chatterjee 2008: 178).

What we need today is an 'interventionist historiography of ideas' which will critically examine these theoretical positions from different vantage points and will prevent them from becoming static categories. Each new reading of a text dislodges it from our taken-for-granted conceptions about it and leads us to the production of new knowledge about that text. This is the only way in which we can ensure the continuity of the existing frameworks of ideas. In the concluding remark of this study, I would also like to point out that not many attempts have been made to understand and critically examine the vernacular traditions of poets, either. The reason for this may be the undue importance that we have accorded to Sanskrit intellectual tradition in the reconstruction of India's cultural past, since the beginning of the colonial period to date. Thapar observes,

> They [colonial masters] saw India only as a Hindu and Sanskrit civilization, so they set aside the numerous chronicles written largely in Persian by court poets and chronicles of Turkish, Afghan and Mughal rulers. They were regarded as alien to Indian civilization, even though their contents concerned Indian society and politics and the people whom they wrote about had settled in India to become part of Indian society . . . Hindu and Sanskrit elements were highlighted as the contribution of India to world history and the presence of other religious and linguistic cultures such as Buddhism and Jainism or even Islam as it evolved in India were barely recognized in terms of constructing Indian civilization. (2002: 1)

The identification of the Sanskrit *kāvyaśāstra* tradition with India's tradition of poetics will give us only a blinkered perception of it. In our contemporary research about the ancient *kāvyaśāstra* tradition, we should necessarily pay due attention to the works of *kāvyaśāstra* in the vernacular languages, such as *Tolkāppiyam* in Tamil, *Līlātilakam* in Malayāḷam, *Kavirājamārga* in Kannada,

Kavipriya in Brajbhāṣa, etc. Instead of merely reproducing the canonical conception of these texts, what we should focus on is the continuum of these intellectual traditions by reading these texts from different vantage points.

Notes

Introduction: Mapping the Field

1 For a detailed reading of the term Sanskrit cosmopolis, read Pollock's introduction to *The Language of the Gods in the World of Men* (12–19).

2 For a detailed reading on the Junagarh inscription, see (*Epigraphia Indica*; VIII 36–49).

3 According to Salomon, 'This is the first long inscription recorded entirely in more or less standard Sanskrit, as well as the first extensive record in the poetic style' (89).

4 Bhāmaha refers to a few literary theoreticians who antedate him by using such words as *anye*, *apare*, *kecit*. See, I.13,24; II.4,57; III.4; IV.12; I.14,31; II.6,8; III.4; IV.6; II.2,37,93; III.55. Medhāvin is the only literary theoretician he refers to by name. See, II.40,88. Pollock argues that 'there is no reason to think that major works from a much earlier period have been lost' (2003: 89).

5 The word *nāṭya* in Sanskrit means dramatic representation and *śāstra* means the systematic study of a body of knowledge. So the word *nāṭyaśāstra* means the systematic study of dramatic representation.

6 *Āṅgika abhinaya* is acting through limbs and face. *Vācika abhinaya* is acting through verbal language. *Āhārya* is the expression through make-up and costume and *sāttvika abhinaya* is acting through the presentation of emotions. These are called the four ways of acting by Bharata.

7 Other than *kāvya*, the term *sāhitya* is also used to refer to literary prose and poetry. However, the term *sāhitya*, according to Pollock, is often used to signify *kāvya* as an object of theoretical reflection (2003: 46).

8 Although many works in the *nāṭyaśāstra* tradition contain deliberations on poetic language, *nāṭyaśāstra*'s primary focus is drama. For example, in his *Nāṭyaśāstra*, Bharata's reflections on literary language are very minimal, compared to the amount of attention he pays to the structure of dramatic performance on stage. In *Nāṭyaśāstra*, only Chapters 15 and 18 deal with poetic language. Pollock also says that although the idea of *rasa* was an important

point of discussion in *Nāṭyaśāstra* and was well known to literary critics from Bhāmaha onwards, none of the literary theoreticians until Udbhaṭa considered it to be a criterion of literariness or an independent category. For them, '*rasa* was clearly subordinate to and therefore easily subsumed under a larger discourse on figures; it did not constitute the heart of literariness' (2016: 10–11).

9 Kalhaṇa's observation about the revival of love for knowledge during the reign of Avantivarman bears testimony to it.

> The minister Śūra by honouring learned men with a seat in the prince's Sabha, caused learning, whose flow had been interrupted, to descend [again] upon this land. The scholars, who were granted great fortunes and high honours, proceeded to the Sabha in vehicles (litters) worthy of kings. Muktagaṇa, Śivasvamin, the poet Ānandavardhana and Ratnākara obtained fame during the reign of Avantivarman. (1900: 189)

10 For a detailed reading of Ānandavardhana's contribution to Sanskrit poetics in Kashmir, see *The Teleology of Poetics in Medieval Kashmir* by Lawrence J. McCrea.

11 Following her husband's death, she placed her son Abhimanyu on the throne and ruled on his behalf for some time. To secure her own safety, she fomented rivalry between the military and political factions of the country. Not long after his coming of age, Didda's son Abhimanyu passed away. After Abhimanyu, Didda placed three of her grandsons on the throne, and they were all murdered after enjoying brief stints of sovereignty. Finally from 980 to 1003 CE, she assumed power in her own right and eventually left the kingdom to her nephew whom she had apparently chosen after careful examination.

12 *saṃskrtam prākrtaṃ cānyadapabhraṃśa ititridhā*|| (*Kāvyālaṅkāra* I.16.). According to Pollock, the choice of a trans-local language for the production of *kāvya* capacitated Sanskrit to cater to a wider audience (2006: 103).

13 Resembling the cardinal conceptions of Sanskrit literary theoreticians about the ontology of *kāvya*, the unknown author of *Līlātilakam* observes, 'Maṇipravāḷam has *śarīra* [body], *doṣa*s [poetic faults], *guṇa* [poetic excellence], *alaṅkāra*s [figures of speech], and *ātma* [soul]. The

body is composed of *bhāṣa* and Sanskrit; the *doṣa*s are cacophony, etc.; the *guṇa*s are sweetness, etc.; *alaṅkāra*s are *upamā*, *anuprāsa*, etc.; *rasas* like *śṛṅgāra* make its soul' (119). Out of the eight *śilpa*s (chapters) in *Līlātilakam*, all the other *śilpa*s except the first three are very much founded on Sanskrit poetics. The fourth *śilpa* deals with *doṣa*s or poetic faults; the fifth one with *guṇa*s or poetic merits; the sixth one with *śabdālaṅkāra*s or the ornaments of sound; the seventh one with *arthālaṅkāra*s or the ornament of sound and the eighth one with *rasa*s or aesthetic emotion. Not only *Līlātilakam*, but all the other works that dealt with the literary language Maṇipravāḷam very much adhered to the poetics of Sanskrit (Freeman 2003: 449).

14 *Kavirājamārga* is the earliest work on poetics from Kannada literature.

15 For a review of all the works in Sanskrit poetics ever published in India, see *An Annotated Bibliography of the Alaṃkāraśāstra* by Timothy C. Cahill. A note of warning should be sounded now: though Sanskrit *kāvyaśāstra* texts continued to get produced in the 19th century, the amount of original thought that went into these texts remains to be determined. Any categorical observation about the originality of these texts in terms of their interaction with the tradition requires a great amount of work. However, one thing we can say for certain is that none of these texts composed during the colonial period could become landmarks in the history of Sanskrit poetics as Jagannātha's *Rasagaṅgādhara* or Appayya Dīkṣita's *Kuvalayānanda* could do in the previous epoch.

16 This is primarily because of the change in the idea of literariness. First, by the 20th century, the traditional ontological notions about literature (to which Sanskrit *kāvyaśāstra* greatly conformed) started undergoing a radical transformation, and the style and language of literary works became similar to everyday speech. By now, the status of Sanskrit poetics got reduced to that of a museum piece, representing the glory of early Indian literature.

17 We should not think that with the arrival of Western literature, the old Sanskritic model of composing poems abruptly ended. It continued to remain active even in the mid-20th century, although the style of literary language also started changing. Keshavan Veluthat observes,

> Even the works of later writers such as Kaṇṇaśśan, Ceṟuśśēri and Tuñcatt Eḻuttacchan, which are 'Keraḷabhāṣāgānams', use

this amalgamated language. The still later Śrīkṛṣṇacaritam calls itself Maṇipravāḷam although it is very different from the early Maṇipravāḷam texts in terms of content. The term Maṇipravāḷam was a synonym for Malayalam [literature] even in nineteenth and early twentieth centuries. For instance, Naḷini of Kumaran Asan, which can be said to have inaugurated the modern in Malayalam poetry, used to be called a Maṇipravāḷa-kāvyaṃ! The late nineteenth century translation of *Abhijñānaśākuntala* into Malyalam by Keraḷa Varma Valiya Kōil Taṁpurān was known as Maṇipravāḷa Śākuntaḷam (1898). Statements such as 'Our Malayalam language that is Maṇipravāḷam' (maṇipravāḷam enna nammuṭe malayāḷabhāṣa) were very common in the twentieth century. (2013: 1)

18 Devy's observation that Sanskrit *kāvyaśāstra* cannot be employed to appreciate or interpret modern literary works as the concerns of literature changed over the years is indeed valid. However, his view that we need to eschew Sanskrit *kāvyaśāstra* and create native critical frameworks to appreciate Indian literary works appears to be somewhat flawed. Devy's position is problematic on two grounds. First of all, Devy does not think about any possibility of seeing Sanskrit *kāvyaśāstra* beyond the canonical way these theories have been understood, that is, as an attempt to identify and analyse formal factors that generate literariness in a work of art. Second, Devy's opinion that only a native sensibility can better appreciate the nuances of meaning in *bhāṣa* literature is also a fallacious position. The assumption here seems to be that a literary work inherently possesses an 'authentic' meaning which can be retrieved, provided we have the 'right' literary and critical abilities. A literary work will not have a single authentic meaning or inherent literariness. Therefore, it would be erroneous to argue that a critical theory, embedded in the literary traditions of the work under scrutiny, can effectively understand it more than any other critical tool.

Chapter 1: Beyond the Canon

1 It is significant to note that Sanskrit *kāvyaśāstra* in its canonical form is very much similar to Russian Formalism in the Western critical praxis. Formalism, like Sanskrit literary science, sees literature as a special mode

of language, distinctly different from ordinary language. According to Eagleton, 'The Formalists, saw literary language as . . . a "special" kind of language, in contrast to the "ordinary" language we commonly use' (1996: 4). For Formalists, say Abrams and Harpham,

> [t]he central function of ordinary language is to communicate to auditors a message, or information, by reference to the world existing outside of language . . . The linguistics of literature differs from the linguistics of practical discourse because its laws are oriented toward producing the distinctive features that formalists call literariness. (2012: 142)

Jan Mukarovsky in his 'Standard Language and Poetic Language' says that 'poetic language', unlike the ordinary language of everyday life, foregrounds its unique nature by pushing communication into the background and inviting the readers' attention to its own unique form (1964: 19). This conception of literature as a special mode of language endorsed by Mukarovsky typifies the view of all Formalist critics about literature. The primary function of these special formal devices, according to Victor Shklovksy, is to 'defamiliarize' or 'estrange' literary language from ordinary use of language. Assuming that a literary work has a non-ordinary ontology characterised by the presence of literariness, the Formalist critics were preoccupied with the task of identifying and analysing the special formal devices generating literariness in a work of literature. In the lines cited by Eichenbaum, Roman Jakobson observes: 'The object of study in literature is not literature but "literariness" that is what makes a given work a literary work' (quoted in Eichenbaum 1971: 27). What we should note here is that both the Formalist theoretical position in the West and Sanskrit *kāvyaśāstra* tradition in the East hold an exclusionist view of literature which proposes that only certain uses of language characterised by a special treatment can qualify to become literature.

2 Jayadeva criticises Mammaṭa for treating *alaṅkāra* only as an optional element in *kāvya*. In *Candrāloka*, Jayadeva mockingly says that a person who opines that a composition of sound and sense without *alaṅkāra* is a *kāvya* will maintain that fire is bereft of heat. For Jayadeva's comment, see *Candrāloka* (1932: I.8).

3 In *Sarasvatīkaṇṭhābharaṇa*, Bhoja illustrates the process by which a non-descript expression is made poetic and laden with *rasa* through the figurative deviation of speech. Bhoja says, in the expression 'Hey maiden, why don't you love me who loves you a lot?', we have an ordinary expression that produces only boredom [because it lacks *rasa* or aesthetic emotion]; in 'The God of love, that cruel person, is pitiless to me, but he holds no grudge to you, my pretty-eyed lass', the sense is sophisticated and generates *rasa*. The factors that are instrumental for the creation of *rasa* [the most important distinguishing mark of *kāvya*] are these—a novel idea; non-ordinary, mellifluous expression; beautiful composition; clarity in articulation and meaning that conforms to propriety (1934: 555). Bhoja borrows this example from Daṇḍin's *Kāvyādarśa* (1962: I.63–64). For Daṇḍin's use of this passage, see (1962: I.63–64). Similarly, in *Śṛṅgāraprakāśa*, Bhoja lists 12 rules governing the combination of signifier (*śabda*) and signification (*artha*) in the production of poetic language (I.2). Of these 12 principles, while the first eight are common to many other forms of language, the last four are unique to the linguistic body of *kāvya*. These four characteristics that Bhoja exclusively reserves for *kāvya* include the presence of poetic qualities, figures of speech, aesthetic emotion and the absence of poetic faults (144).

4 Samudrabandha, a 12th-century Sanskrit critic from Kerala, is known for his commentary on Ruyyaka's *Alaṅkārasarvasva*. Although Samudrabhandha mentions only three distinct elements of which the presences make *kāvya* a distinct use of language, we can find other literary theoreticians referring to many other textual devices such as *aucitya*, *rasa* and so on.

5 The term *alaṅkāra*, apart from denoting what we today call figures of speech, was broadly used to signify all the beautifying elements in *kāvya*. For a detailed reading in this respect, see I.36 and V.66 of *Kāvyālaṅkāra*; II.1 of *Kāvyādarśa* and I.1.2 of *Kāvyālaṅkārasūtravrtti*.

6 Bhāmaha employs the term *alaṅkāra* in the wider sense of the term, i.e., poetic beauty.

7 Ānandavardhana in *Dhvanyāloka* repeats this idea (1990: 3.36).

8 K.C. Pandey, in his *Comparative Aesthetics*, summarises the importance of deviant utterance in the theory of Bhāmaha. According to him, 'It is this very *lakṣaṇā* spoken of as *vakrokti* that is represented to be the most essential element of all poetic embellishments' (499). Vijayavardhana

also holds the same opinion. For Vijayavardhana's comment, see *Outlines of Sanskrit Poetics* (2010: 29).

9 Vāmana borrows this example from Patañjali's *Mahābhāshya.* Abhinavagupta also reproduces a fragment of this quotation (*daśa dādimāni ṣaḍ apūpaḥ*) in his *Locana* on Ānandavardhana's *Dhvanyāloka*. See (*Dhvānyaloka* edited by Ingalls *kārika* 1.4 b). He identifies 10 *artha-guṇa*s and 10 *śabda-guṇa*s and 31 *alaṅkāra*s that confer literariness upon a text. Vāmana is the first literary theoretician to classify *guṇa*s into *artha-guṇa*s and *śabda-guṇa*s.

10 Though Vāmana opines that the body of *kāvya* is characterised by sound and sense adorned by *guṇa*s and *alaṅkāra*s (3), he privileges *guṇa*s over *alaṅkāras*. According to him, it is *guṇa*s such as *ojas* and *prasāda* that are responsible for the unique nature of *kāvya*. The function of *alaṅkāra*, on the other hand, is only to enhance the beauty of *kāvya* which is already beautified by the presence of *guṇa*s (90). Though there is a shift of focus in Vāmana's theory from *alaṅkāra* to *guṇa*, the idea that *kāvya* is a supra-normal entity remains unchanged.

11 In a classroom experiment, Fish presented before his students a list of random words and told them that it was a religious poem that they should interpret. The students who had been studying 17th century religious poetry, began to notice biblical references and all sorts of structural and semantic cohesion in the text, thereby giving the text 'literariness' and meaning. For Fish's experiment, see Chapter 14, 'How to Recognize a Poem When You See One' in *Is There a Text in This Class?* (1980).

12 For a detailed reading of the approaches that advocate the employment of Sanskrit *kāvyaśāstra* to evaluate the literary merit of a work, see Krishna Rayan's '*Rasa-Dhvani* and Present-day Literary Theory and Criticism', K. Ayyappa Paniker's 'The Renovation of Rasa-theory' ('Rasasidhānta navīkaraṇam') (1999), Sivarudrappa and Rao's 'Literary Criticism in Indian Poetics' (1985), K. Satchidanandan's 'Dilemmas of Indian Literary Criticism' (2014), Ramlal Joshi and Dignesh Mehta's 'The Critical Process' (1985), M.S. Kushwaha's 'The Contemporary Relevance of Indian Aesthetics: Some Reflections' (1992), etc.

13 According to Gramsci, the term 'hegemony' refers to that social situation in which the dominant force in a society imposes their values, beliefs,

explanations and mores upon the subordinate subjects in such a way that they willingly consent to the ideology of the dominant force, and accept it as authentic and natural, as opposed to seeing it as the artificial construct of the dominant group. Gramsci defines hegemony in the following words, [It is] the spontaneous consent given by the great masses of the population to the general direction imposed on social life by the dominant fundamental group; this consent is historically caused by the prestige (and consequent confidence) which the dominant group enjoys because of its position and function in the world of production (2000: 306–307). For a detailed reading of Gramsci's concept of hegemony, see the article 'Intellectuals and Education'. Gramsci borrowed the concept of hegemony from Marx who noted that 'the ruling ideas of each age have ever been the ideas of its ruling class' (Engels and Marx 2005).

14 Bernard Harrison neatly summarises these ideological postulations concerning the idea of a text. He says,

> (a) No text has a determinate meaning.
> (b) A text, though it may refer to other texts, refers to nothing extra-textual.
> (c) Equally legitimate interpretations of a text may be incompatible with one another, or just have nothing in common.
> (d) Since a text gives no access to the conscious state of its author, it gives no access to authorial consciousness, *tout court,* and therefore cannot be taken as in any sense a *communication* from author to reader.
> (e) The job of the critic is not to explain what a text means, but to elaborate it into a new text. (1991: 123)

15 The following passage from *Maitreya Upaniṣad* succinctly summarises the 'essence' of Brahman which defies all ontological categorisations.

> In the beginning, Brahman was all this. He was one, and infinite; infinite in the East, infinite in the South, infinite in the West, infinite in the North, above and below and everywhere infinite. East and the other regions do not exist for him, or across, or below, or above. The Highest Self is not to be fixed, he is unlimited, unborn, not to be reasoned about, not to be conceived. (318)

Indicating the irreducibility of Brahman, *Kenopaniṣad* also says that Brahman is 'what none can comprehend with the mind' (*'yan manasā na manucite'*; 13), 'what none can see with the eyes' (*'yaccakṣusā na paśyati'*; 13), 'what none can hear by the ears' (*'yacchotreṇa na śruṇoti'*; 14) and 'what none can breathe with breath' (*'yat prāṇena na prāṇanti'*; 14).

Chapter 2: *Avivakṣita-vācya*-dhvani and the Restructuring of Conventional Semantic Ambit

1 By revealing the true nature of *dhvani*, not only does Ānanda aim to answer his critics but also plans to delight the heart of sensitive readers (*sahrdayamanḥ prītaye*; 47).

2 On the basis of the presence of *dhvani*, Ānanda divides *kāvya* into three categories, namely *dhvani kāvya*, *guṇibhūta-vyaṅgya-kāvya* and *citra-kāvya*. *Dhvani-kāvya* is the *kāvya* where poetic suggestion predominantes. The second variety, that is *guṇibhūta-vyaṅgya-kāvya,* is that kind of *kāvya* where the suggested elements always remains subordinate to what is explicitly stated. According to Ānandavardhana, explicitly mentioning what is previously suggested ruins the charm of suggestion. If the suggested element is explicitly stated later in the poem, then the poem will be relegated to the position of *guṇibhūta-vyaṅgya-kāvya*. According to Ānanda, the subordination of the suggested element 'to the principal sense of the sentence is like a king's following after his servant in the servant's wedding procession' (3.34 *A*). Standing in contrast to *dhvani-kāvya* is what Ānanda calls *citra-kāvya*. According to Ānandavardhana, a type of poetry which looks beautiful because of its novelties of literal sense and expression, but fails to suggest a *rasa* or a fact or a thing as its final meaning is called *citra-kāvya*. For Ānanda, it is not real poetry but just an imitation of poetry like a *citra* or painting (3.41–42 *K*).

3 In *Śabarabhāṣya*, the *mīmāṃsā* philosopher Śabarasvāmin (2 CE) presents a *pūrvapakṣa* view which states that the relationship between a signifier and signified is not natural, but conventional. The *pūrvapakṣa* view says that had there been any natural relation between a *pada* and *padārtha*, the utterance of signifiers would have left an actual impact upon the speaker, just as the real objects referred to by these words do in actual life. That is to say, the utterance of the word 'razor' would have cut out our mouths or

reference to the word 'sweet' would have filled our mouths with sweetness (1923: I.18). In *Nyāyasūtra*, Akṣapāda Gautama (6 BCE?) also asserts that a particular signification is obtained from a signifier by way of convention (*sāmayika*) (39). Had there been any natural relation between a signifier and a signified, Gautama says, the same word would have been used to denote a particular idea across different linguistic communities (1913: 39). Pakṣilasvāmin Vātsyāyana (450 CE), in *Nyāyasūtrabhāṣya*, subscribes to Gautama's view and says that a signifier is not naturally (*svbhāvika*) attached to a signified. According to him, the words are employed to represent certain ideas as per the arbitrary wishes of the sages, nobles and barbarians. If a word had naturally conveyed its signification, words would not have varied across different linguistic communities (1896: 94). Vātsyāyana also says that convention which binds a *pada* with *padārtha* has a restrictive nature (1896: 93).

4 The expression *vivakṣitānya-paravācya* literally means 'the literal meaning (*vivakṣita*) understood in a different way (*anyaparavācya*)'. In *vivakṣitānya-paravācya-dhvani*, the literal meaning, although intended, moves onto suggest something which is not explicitly presented such as a *rasa* (aesthetic emotion), an *alaṅkāra* (a figure of speech) or a *vastu* (a fact) (565). *Vivakṣitānya-paravācya* is broadly divided into two—*saṃlakṣya-krama-vyaṅgya* and *asaṃlakṣya-krama-vyaṅgya*—on the basis of whether we are conscious of the succession from the literal meaning to the suggested element. In *asaṃlakṣya-krama-vyaṅgya*, we are not conscious of the movement from the literal to the suggested (212–213). Only *rasa-dhvani* falls within the ambit of *asaṃlakṣya-krama-vyaṅgya*. In *saṃlakṣya-krama-vyaṅgya*, which is also known as *anuraṇana-rūpa-vyaṅgya-dhvani* (suggested sense appearing like a reverberation), we are conscious of the movement that takes place from the literal meaning to the suggested meaning. In other words, first we perceive the literal sense; then after a momentary interval, the suggested sense dawns on us. *Saṃlakṣya-krama-vyaṅgya* is divided into two varieties such as *śabda-śakti-mūla* and *artha-śakti-mūla* (338). *Śabda-śakti-mūla* is that variety of *dhvani* where a figure of speech is implied, without being directly expressed, by a word or a set of words (292). In *artha-śakti-mūla-dhvani*, words, in addition to their literal sense, suggest a new meaning by the power of primary meaning (311).

5 There are generally three conditions which are necessary for the transfer of meaning in secondary usage such as (1) the impossibility of the conventional meaning in the given context, (2) some kind of relation between the conventional meaning of the signifier and the new meaning the signifier has attained and finally (3) the sanction for the abandonment of the conventional meaning by popular usage or some other definite motive for the transfer of meaning (Raja 2000: 232). Among these three conditions, the first two are unanimously accepted by all writers. But regarding the last one, there exists a rift between the earlier grammarians and the literary critics. While the earlier grammarians are of the view that the connection between the signifier and the new (secondary) meaning should be sanctioned by popular usage, the *ālaṅkārika*s are ready to accept even the secondary usages that are unconventional. For example, Mammaṭa, in *Kāvyaprakāśa*, says that this relation between the conventional meaning and the new meaning need not be sanctioned by popular usage. If that were the case, Mammaṭa notes, the sentence *mañcāḥ krośanti* (benches cry; here, benches signify the people who sit on it) would not have made any sense, as the relation between the persons who sit on the bench and the bench is temporary and not sanctioned by popular usage (1966: 24).

6 For Ānandavardhana, secondary usage (*guṇavṛtti* or *bhākta*) functions only as an *upalakṣaṇā* (adventitious mark) of *dhvani* (1990: 1.19). An *upalakṣaṇā* denotes a characteristic mark that helps us define a thing only temporarily under certain conditions. For example, 'the first house east of the lake' can be the *lakṣaṇā* (here, the word *lakṣaṇā* means a characteristic mark) of a washerman's house. An *upalakṣaṇā* of this house would be 'the house on the roof of which a crow is sitting'. This is an *upalakṣaṇā* because the crow that sits on the house may fly away at any moment and hence it cannot be considered a permanent marker to identify the washerman's house (67). According to Ānanda, if we say that secondary usage is a *lakṣaṇā* or a characteristic mark of *dhvani*, we will court what he calls the fallacy of 'too broad' (189). The fallacy of 'too borad' denotes a definition that includes items that should not have been included in it. For example, if we define an apple as anything which is red and round, that will eventuate in the fallacy of 'too broad' because all that

is red and round cannot be an apple. (The planet Mars is also red and round. According to the aforesaid definition, Mars should also be considered an apple. Therefore, this definition is faulty.) These examples point to the fact that *avivakṣita-vācya-dhvani* does not occur in all the instances where secondary usage occurs. Therefore secondary usage cannot be identified with *avivakṣita-vācya* variety of *dhvani*. If a secondary usage needs to become an *avivakṣita-vācya-dhvani*, it should operate on a signifier in such a way that it produces a new meaning which is not yet a part of the linguistic convention.

Chapter 3: *Aucitya*: A Mechanism of Control

1 Particularly important is the article 'The Social Aesthetic and Sanskrit Literary Theory' (2001) by Pollock where Pollock highlights the question of morality in Sanskrit poetics.

2 Foucault defines the term discourse differently in different works. Foucault in his *The Archaeology of Knowledge* talks about the different shades of the term 'discourse' in his philosophy:

> Instead of gradually reducing the rather fluctuating meaning of the word 'discourse,' I believe I have in fact added to its meaning: treating it sometimes as the general domain of all statements, sometimes as an individualizable group of statements, and sometimes as a regulated practice that accounts for a number of statements. (1972: 80)

In the present discussion, I stick to Foucault's definition of discourse as 'a regulated practice that accounts for a number of statements' (80). In this context, the term discourse means a set of rules that govern the actions of individuals and institutions in any society. Iara Lessa who defines Foucault's idea of discourse from this perspective says that the term discourse denotes 'systems of thoughts composed of ideas, attitudes, courses of action, beliefs, and practices that systematically construct the subjects and the worlds of which they speak' (2006: 285).

3 For a detailed reading of how *aucitya* pervades the entire history of Sanskrit literary science, see Raghavan (1942: 194–252), Krishnamoorthy (1964: 114–136) and Sastri (1945: 28).

4 See respectively Chapter IV of Bhāmaha's *Kāvyālaṅkāra* (1998), I.62-67 of *Kāvyādarśa of Daṇḍin* (1962), Chapters II and III of Vāmana's *Kāvyālaṅkārasūtravrtti*, Chapter VII of Viśvanātha's *Sāhityadarpaṇa* (2016), Chapter III of Mahimabhaṭṭa's *Vyaktiviveka* (1901). Mahimabhaṭṭa divides the entire poetic *doṣas* into *śabdaucitya* and *arthaucitya* (1901: 37).

5 A case in point which shows *Nāṭyaśāstra*'s influence in connection with the idea of *aucitya* upon the writings of later writers is their reproduction of Bharata's representation of *aṣṭanāyika* (eight kinds of heroines in eight different emotional situations). Bharata's concept of *aṣṭanāyika* was highly influential not only for drama but also for literature, music and painting. For instance, works like Dhanika and Dhanañjaya's *Daśarūpaka*, Viśvanātha *Sāhityadarpaṇa*, Bhoja's *Śṛṅgāraprakāśa*, etc., follow this tradition of setting the models of various kinds of heroines for creative writers. Bhānudatta's description of *nāyikās* in *Rasataraṅgiṇī* and *Rasamañjarī* are obviously inspired by Bharata's description of heroines in *Nāṭyaśāstra*. It also influenced a lot of *Kāmaśāstra* texts such as *Kuṭṭāṇīmata*, *Pancāsāyaka*, *Anaṅgaraṅga*, etc. Keśavadas's *Rasikapriya* in Hindi also draws upon Bharata's notion of *aṣṭanāyikas*. The medieval paintings such as *ragamālika* also got influenced by this description of heroines.

6 A case in point is the observation of Ānandavardhana. Ānanda observes,

> Thus, if we assign a type of love to characters of the upper class by recourse to what is appropriate to the lower class, how ridiculous will be the result! Even in India what is appropriate in love differs according to the three classes of men (*uttamā*, *madhyamā* and *adhamā*). (1990: 3.10–14 b)

7 See, the second chapter (*prakāśa*) of *Daśarūpaka* (1941) where Dhanañjaya talks in detail about the qualities of a hero, various categories of the hero, the characteristics of the helpers of the hero, antagonists, different kinds of heroines, the qualities that are to be attributed to the side-kicks of a heroine, etc.; the second chapter (*prakaraṇa*) of Vidyānātha's *Pratāparudrīya* (1933) is concerned with the representation of heroes and heroines; in Bhoja's *Śṛṅgāraprakāśa* (1963), see Chapters 21 and 32 which talk about the representation

of heroes and heroines; in *Rasamañjarī* (2009), see the description on *nāyikā* and *nāyaka*.

8 Ānanda's observation on the representation of sexual union is also worth mentioning here. He says,

> Accordingly, whether in the literature of performance or in poetry which is not performed, the description of vulgar sexual enjoyment between characters of the upper class, kings and ladies, is highly indecent, just like the description of the sexual enjoyment of our parents. Precisely, the same charge appears within the sphere of the gods. Furthermore, sexual intercourse is not the only form of love-in-enjoyment (saṃbhoga-śṛṅgāra). Other forms such as the interchange of glances and the like are possible and can be used in writing of upper-class characters. Thus that which is appropriate to the character is to be followed in treating of sexual desire (rati) just as of energy. (1990: 3.10–14 b A)

9 This is a tendency which begins as early as by Bhāmaha and Daṇḍin. See *āgamavirodha* (the poetic fault arising out of the conflict with the *dharmaśāstra*), *nyāyavirodha* (the poetic blemish that arises out of the statements contradicting the observations in śāstras related to *dharma*, *artha* and *kāma*), *kālavirodha* (the inappropriateness of time), *kalāvirodha* (the poetic fault arising out of the lack of technical knowledge about arts), *deśavirodha* (inappropriateness of place), etc., by Bhāmaha (1998: IV.33–40) and Daṇḍin (1962: III.165–185).

10 Stephen Greenblatt's concept of self-fashioning which he introduced in his *Renaissance Self-fashioning: From More to Shakespeare* is a very useful conceptual framework here. Greenblatt employed the concept of self-fashioning to designate the process by which the upper class in Renaissance England fashioned their subjectivity after the socially accepted standards about the public persona of the noblemen and women propagated through art and literature, especially through Shakespearean dramas. According to Greenblatt, in the 16th century, there appeared 'an increased self-consciousness about the fashioning of human identity as a manipulable, artful process' (2). He opines that 'It [art] offered men the

power to shape their world, calculate the probabilities, and master the contingent, and it implied that human character itself could be similarly fashioned, with an eye to audience and effect' (162). Even though this process is termed self-fashioning, the subjects of the upper class did not have absolute agency in self-fashioning themselves. In other words, the outcome of self-fashioning was predetermined. When the nobility self-fashioned themselves, they did it in accordance with the prescribed requirements of society. In his epilogue to *Renaissance Self-fashioning*, Greenblatt says,

> In all my texts and documents, there were, so far as I could tell, no moments of pure, unfettered subjectivity; indeed, the human subject itself began to seem remarkably unfree, the ideological product of the relations of power in a particular society. Whenever I focused sharply upon a moment of apparently autonomous self-fashioning, I found not an epiphany of identity freely chosen but a cultural artefact. If there remained traces of free choice, the choice was among possibilities whose range was strictly delineated by the social and ideological system in force. (256)

What Greenblatt says is that self-fashioning is not about the way in which people fashion themselves—rather, it is about the way in which the dominant socio-political forces instigate the nobility in England to fashion themselves in accordance with certain socially accepted models. Along the same lines, *Kāvyaśāstra* in Sanskrit was also providing the create writers with the same grammar of representation so that the readers will have an ideal and imitable model for refashioning.

Chapter 4: *Vakrokti* as a Resistance to *Svabhāva*

1 It is significant to note that although Bhāmaha is the first literary critic to employ the term *vakrokti*, Bharata had already talked about it in his *Nāṭyaśāstra*. Instead of *vakrokti*, he used the term *lakṣaṇā* to refer to what Bhāmaha would later call *vakrokti*. According to K.C. Pandey, '*Vakrokti* is not a production of the originality of Bhāmaha. According to the information available from the existing literature he is indebted to Bharata'

(2008: 495). For a detailed reading of Bharata's idea of *lakṣaṇā*, see the 16th chapter of *Nāṭyaśāstra* where Bharata talks about 36 varieties of *lakṣaṇās*.

2 Daṇḍin, on the other hand, opines that the plain expressions such as 'the sun has set, the moon shines, the birds are flying back to their nest', etc., can achieve the status of *alaṅkāra* in *kāvya*. See Daṇḍin's *Kāvyādarśa* (1962: II.244).

3 *Śleṣa-vakrokti* is *vakrokti* based on a pun, whereas *kāku-vakrokti* is *vakrokti* based on the tone of voice. According to Rudraṭa, 'A sentence uttered in one sense by a speaker and then taken in another sense by a listener—because of the double meaning of the words—is called a *śleṣa vakratā* (*vakratā* of pun)' (1886: 15). Sometimes because of a change in the speaker's intonation, there is a change in the meaning of a sentence. It is called *kāku vakratā* or *vakratā* of tone (16).

4 This short poem portrays Goddess Pārvatī's attempts to break up with her husband Śiva, and Śiva's attempts to assuage her anger through the skilful employment of deviant utterance. Śiva playfully evades Pārvatī's complaints by intentionally taking them in a sense which Pārvatī does not intend, thereby dragging their conversation to the point of Pārvatī finally reconciling with Śiva. Other poems modelled on Ratnākara's skilful use of deviant utterance in *Vakroktipañcaśikā* include Śivarāma's *Lakṣmī-sarasvatī-saṃvāda* and the anonymous *Rambhā-śuka-saṃvāda* and *Girijā-kamala-vivāda*. *Lakṣmī-sarasvatī-saṃvāda* portrays the verbal fencing between Lakṣmī and Sarasvatī—the rival wives of Viṣṇu and Śiva; *Rambhā-śuka-saṃvāda* deals with the dialogue between the ascetic Śuka and the celestial woman Raṃbhā who has come to earth to seduce Śuka, and *Girijā-kamalā-vivāda* is in the form of a dialogue between Pārvatī and Lakṣmī.

5 Quoted in Bronner and McCrea's 'To Be or Not to Be Śiśupāla: Which Version of the Key Speech in Māgha's Great Poem Did He Really Write?' (2012).

6 For a detailed reading of these five varities, read Hedge's *The Concept of Vakrokti in Sanskrit Poetics* (2009).

7 *Pada-pūrvārtha-vakratā* is again divided into nine categories namely *rūḍhī-vaicitrya-vakratā* (a deviant use of the primary meaning of words in such a way that words abandon their primary meaning to signify a new meaning which is not conventionally associated with them),

paryāya-vakratā (artistic deviation through the synonyms of a word), *upacāra-vakratā* (artistic deviation through secondary usage), *viśeṣaṇa-vakratā* (artistic deviation through adverbs, adjectives and epithets), *saṃvrti-vakratā* (artistic deviation through concealment), *vrtti-vakratā* (artistic deviance through the use of compounds), *bhāva-vakratā* (artistic deviance wherein an activity yet to be completed is presented as already completed), *liṅga-vaicitrya-vakratā* (deviant use of gender) and *kriyā-vaicitrya-vakratā* (artistic deviance through verb roots) (2009: 231–295). *Liṅga-vaicitrya-vakratā* has three subdivisions, namely, the use of words having the same meaning, yet belonging to different gender categories; the employment of a specific gender for an object, although other genders are applicable, and the preference of feminine gender for an object, despite the possibility of other genders (287–291). Similarly *kriyā-vaicitrya-vakratā* also has five varieties namely *karturatyanta-raṅgatva-vakratā* (non-literal expression of an idea through the performance of an action which is in some way associated with that idea), *kartāntara-vaicitrya-vakratā* (attributing to an object an ability which the object is unable to perform), *kriyā-viśeṣaṇa-vaicitrya-vakratā* (deviant utterance through the employment of adverbs), *upacāra-manohārita-vakratā* (metaphorical superimposition of a quality upon an object) and *karmādi-saṃvrti-vakratā* (concealment of an action or direct object) (II.4–25).

8 *Pada-parārtha-vakratā* has six subdivisions such as *kāla-vaicitrya-vakratā* (deviant use of tense), *karaka-vakrutā* (artistic deviation through the reversal of subject, instrument of action, case, etc.), *saṃkhyā-vakratā* (artistic deviation of numbers), *puruṣa-vakratā* (artistic deviation through the transposition of *uttamā*, *madhyamā* and *pradhamā*), *upagraha-vakratā* (artistic deviation through the skilful use of *ātmanepad* and *parasmaipad* forms) and *pratyaya-vakratā* (artistic deviation through affixes) (2009: II.26–34).

9 *Prakaraṇa-vakratā* is divided into 10 categories such as *pariṇāma-gopana-vakratā* (artistic deviation through the incorporation of new episodes to show the true nature of characters), *utpādya-lāvaṇya-vakratā* (artistic deviation through the addition or deletion of episodes in an already existing story), *upakāryopakāra-kartṛtva-vakratā* (artistic deviation through the representation of conventional themes in a new

manner), *abhidheyāvarttana-vakratā* (deviant representation of the same *rasa* in different ways), *kathopakāraka-vastu-vinyāsa-vakratā* (artistic deviance through the invention of a new plot in a story in such a way that it remains crucial to the total *rasa* and the story of the work), *kathā-vaicitrya-vakratā* (artistic deviance through the incorporation of an otherwise insignificant incident to present the story in a strikingly new way), *aṅgirasa-niṣyanta-vakratā* (artistic deviance through the incorporation of subordinate emotions to present the story in a deviant form), *vastvantara-vaicitrya-vakratā* (artistic deviance wherein the poet invents an incident in such a way that it indirectly remains significant to the main plot), *prakaraṇāntara-vakratā* (artistic deviance through the incorporation of a play within a play) and *aṅgāṅgi-sāṃgatya-vakratā* (artistic deviation through the incorporation of an otherwise staple or insipid moment in a delightful manner) (2009: IV.1–15).

10 *Prabandha-vakratā* has seven varieties namely *rasāntara-vinyāsa-vakratā* (artistic deviation to change the generally accepted *rasa* of a well-known story), *nāyakolkkarṣa-nibandhana-vakratā* (artistic deviation to make a story [often a tragic story] end on a happy note), *prāsaṃgika-kathāsāra-nibandhana-vakratā* (artistic deviance wherein the poet transforms what is generally deemed to be a 'digression from the main story' into an interesting event in such a way that it becomes inevitable for the main story), *aneka-pḥala-sambatti-vakratā* (artistic deviance to enhance the glory of a hero by showing him achieving a lot of subsidiary feats, besides his main goal), *kāvya-nāma-vakratā* (artistic deviation through appropriate titles), *anyonya-vailakṣaṇya-vakratā* (artistic deviance through the representation of a familiar story in a new way) and *nayopadeśa-vakratā* (artistic deviance in teaching moral lessons) (2009: IV.16–26).

11 Kuntaka repeatedly says that *vakrokti* is an *alaṅkāra*. For example, see this verse:

> *ubhāvetāvalaṅkaryau tayoḥ punaralaṅkrtiḥ-*
> *vakroktireva vaidagdhyabhaṅgībhaṇitirucyate*| (91)

Kuntaka subscribes to the traditional view that *kāvya* is primarily a combination of *śabda* and *artha* adorned by *alaṅkāras*. Then, he proceeds to say that what functions as the *alaṅkāra* for *śabda* and *artha* is none other than *vakrokti* (*tayoḥ punralaṅkrtiḥ vakroktireva vaidagdhyabhaṅgībhaṇitirucyate*). In another instance, Kuntaka observes: 'What is this common ornament? "Deviant utterance" is the answer (91) Kuntaka even goes to the extent of calling *Vakroktijīvita* a work on *alaṅkāra*. In the first chapter, he even calls the text an 'ornament' (*tadayamaṛtthaḥ granthasyālaṅkāra ityabhidhānaṃ*; 54). See another observation: *lokottaracamatkārakārivaicitryasidhaye|kāvyasyāyamalaṅkāraḥ ko'pyapūrvo vidhīyate||* (Kuntaka 2009: 53). [Here, I adorn *kāvya* with a rare *alaṅkāra* and introduce an exceptionally striking decorative device.]

12 The opinion of Avantisundarī, the learned wife of the literary theoretician Rājaśekhara, also deserves special mention here. Like Kuntaka and his predecessor Ānandavardhana, Avantisundarī opines that in the world of poetry, the essence of a thing is not stable, since it can be transformed into any form, according to a poet's desire. In the ninth chapter titled *Arthavyāpti* (depth of meaning) of *Kāvyamīmāṃsā*, Rājaśekhara quotes Avantisundarī's words. According to Avantisundarī,

> There is no constant nature of things in poetry. In this poetic world, the nature of a thing is not certain. It is because of poets' words (*ukti*) that it develops certain excellences or faults. Those who wish to worship the moon call it *amrtāmśu* [the nectar-rayed one] and the pessimists who wish to find fault with it name it *doṣākara* [the one who causes distress]. (Rājaśekhara 2000: 139)

13 In *Dhvanyāloka*, Ānandavardhana cites this verse as an example of *arthāntara-saṃkramita-vācya*. For Ānanda's use of this verse, see Ānandavardhana (1990: 2.1b).

14 Ānandavardhana also uses the same example. That is why Abhinava comments on it.

Chapter 5: Towards an Interventionist Intellectual Historiography

1 The equation of identifying the ancient with Hindu and the medieval with Muslim, was based on the fact that many dynasties of the first

period were Hindu, while those of the second were Muslim (Thapar 2002: 18).

2 For example, see '*Rasa* and the Objective Correlative' by Krishna Rayan (1965) where Rayan shows that there is a consensus of opinion between the *rasa* school of Sanskrit literary theory and T.S. Eliot's idea of objective correlative; P.S. Sastri's 'Indian Poetics and New Criticism' (1988) which argues that Cleanth Brooks' 'Paradox' and 'Empson's 'ambiguity' are ideas already anticipated by Kuntaka's *Vakrokti* and R.S. Pathak's 'The Indian Theory of Vakrokti in Relation to the Stylistic Concept of Deviance' (1982), which identifies the interfaces between the canonical reading of Kuntaka's *vakrokti* and the modern Formalistic practice of deviant utterance.

3 This sort of an approach to Sanskrit *kāvyaśāstra* is very much an extension of the position of the early 20th-century Indian historians who attempted to resist the Orientalist view of the colonial historians. The general conception of the European historians such as Vincent Smith writing about Indian history in the 20th century was that Indian society was largely autocratic in nature. The autocratic king unconcerned about the well-being of his subjects was the standard image of an Indian ruler, with a few exceptions like Ashoka and Chandra Gupta II and Akbar. The nationalist historians like R. Mitra, R.G. Bhandarkar, R.C. Dun, A.S. Altekar, U.N. Ghoshal, K.P. Jayaswal, H.C. Raychaudhuri, R.K. Mookherjee, R.C. Majumdar, K.A. Nilakanta Sastri and H.C. Ojha, etc., resisted this Orientalist conception about India's past by attributing to ancient society the virtues that colonial historians were celebrating. They held that the ancient system of the *mantriparishad* (the council of ministers) and the modern British Privy Council share a lot of interfaces with each other. Non-violence was praised as Indian contribution to modern civilisation, and they hailed the Gupta King, Samudragupta, as the Napoleon of India. The idea of nationalism was placed as far back as the 4th century BCE and cited events such as the opposition to Alexander's campaign and the creation of the Mauryan Empire as instances of nationalist sprit.

References

Abhinavagupta. 1990. *Locana*. In *The Dhvanyāloka of Anandavardhana with the Locana of Abhinavagupta*, by Ānandavardhana. Harvard: Harvard University Press.

———. 1992. *Abhinavabhāratī*, Vol. I. In *Nāṭyaśāstra of Bharathamuni*, edited by K. Krishnamoorthy. Oriental Institue Vadodara.

Abrams, M.H. and Geoffrey Galt Harpham. 2012. *A Glossary of Literary Terms*, 10th edn. Wadsworth Cengage Learning.

Amṛtānandayogin. 1949. *Alaṅkārasamgraha*. The Adyar Library.

Ānandavardhana. 1990. *The Dhvanyāloka of Anandavardhana with Lōcana of Abhinavagupta*. Edited by Daniel Ingalls, Jeffry Masson and M.V. Patwardhan. Cambridge: Harvard University.

Andrews, B.R. 1903. 'Habit'. *The American Journal of Psychology*, 14 (2): 121–149.

Anthappayi, K.C. 1939. *Bhasanatakaparishodhana*. St. Marys Orphanage Press.

Ashcroft, Bill and Helen Tiffin. 2002. *The Empire Writes Back*. Routledge.

Barthes, R. 1977. 'Lecture in Inauguration of the Chair of Literary Semiology, College de France, January 7, 1977'. *The MIT Press*, 8: 3–16.

Barthes, R. and R. Howard. 1979. 'Lecture in Inauguration of the Chair of Literary Semiology, Collège de France, January 7, 1977', 3–16. Available at: https://doi.org/10.2307/778222, accessed on 10 July 2023.

Barthes, Roland. 1977. 'The Death of the Author'. In *Image, Music, Text*, translated by Stephen Heath, 143–147. Hill and Wang.

———. 1986. 'From Work to Text'. In *The Rustle of Language*, translated by Richard Howard, 56–64. Hill and Wang.

Bartley, C. 2011. *An Introduction to Indian Philosophy*. Continuum.

Bhāmaha. 1998. *Kāvyālaṅkāra*. Edited by B.N. Sarma and Baldeva Upadhyay. Benares: Chowkhamba Sanskrit Series Office.

Bhānudatta. 2009. *The Bouquet of Rasa and River of Rasa*, edited by Sheldon Pollock. New York: New York University Press.

Bharata. 1997. *Nāṭyaśāstra*, Vol. 1, edited by N.P. Pisharoti. Kerala Sahitya Akademi.

Bharata. 1999. *Nāṭyaśāstra*, Vol. 2, edited by N.P. Pisharoti. Kerala Sahitya Akademi.

Bhoja. 1934. *Sarasvatīkaṇṭhābharaṇa*. Edited by P. Jawaji. Nirnayasagar Press.

———. 1955. *Śṛṅgāraprakāśa*, Vol. I. Edited by G.S. Josyer.

———. 1963. *Śṛṅgāraprakāśa*, Vol. II. Edited by G.S. Josyer.

Bronner, Y. and L. McCrea. 2001. 'The Poetics of Distortive Talk: Plot and Character in Ratnākara's "Fifty Verbal Perversions" (*Vakroktipancāśikā*)'. *Journal of Indian Philosophy*, 29 (4): 435–464. Available at: http://www.jstor.org/stable/23496929, accessed on 1 September 2023.

———. 2012. 'To Be or Not to Be Śiśupāla: Which Version of the Key Speech in Māgha's Great Poem Did He Really Write?' *Journal of the American Oriental Society*, 132 (3): 427–455. Available at: https://doi.org/10.7817/jameroriesoci.132.3.0427, accessed on 5 September 2023.

Bronner, Yigal. 2002. 'What is New and What is Navya: Sanskrit Poetics on the Eve of Colonialism'. *Journal of Indian Philosophy*, 30: 441–462.

———. 2016. 'Understanding Udbhaṭa: The Invention of Kashmiri Poetics in the Jayāpīḍa Moment'. In *Around Abhinavagupta: Aspects of the Intellectual History of Kashmir from the Ninth to the Eleventh Century*, edited by Eli Franco and Isabelle Ratié, 81–147. LIT.

Busch, Allison. 2004. 'The Anxiety of Innovation: The Practice of Literary Science in the Hindi/Riti Tradition'. *Comparative Studies of South Asia, Africa and the Middle East*, 24 (2): 45–59.

Chandran, M. and V.S. Sreenath. 2020. *An Introduction to Indian Aesthetics: History, Theory, and Theoreticians*. Delhi: Bloomsbury.

Chandran, Mini. 2013. 'Reclaiming Lost Territory'. *Economic and Political Weekly*, 48 (40).

Chatterjee, Partha. 2008. 'Critique of Popular Culture'. *Public Culture*, 20 (2): 321–344.

Cuddon, J.A. 1998. *The Penguin Dictionary of Literary Terms and Literary Theory*. Penguin Books.

Daṇḍin. 1962. *Kāvyādarśa of Daṇḍin*. Edited by Premachandra Tarkabagisa. Calcutta: Royal Asiatic Society.

De, S.K. 1961. 'Introduction'. In *Vakroktijīvita*. Firma K.L. Mukhopadhyay.

Deleuze, G. and Guattari Felix. 1983. *Anti-Oedipus: Capitalism and Schizophrenia*, translated by R. Hurley, M. Seem and H.R. Lane. University of Minnesota Press.

Deleuze, G. and Guattari Felix. 2005. *A Thousand Plateaus*, translated by Brian Massumi. University of Minnesota Press.

Derrida, Jaques. 1976. 'Structure Sign and Play: In the Discourse of Human Sciences'. In *Writing and Difference*, by Derrida Jaques. New York: Routledge.

Devy, G.N. 2009. 'After Amnesia: Tradition and Change in Indian Literary Criticism'. In *G.N. Devy Reader*, 1–140. Orient Blackswan.

Dhanañjaya. 1941. *The Daśarūpaka of Dhananjaya with the Commentary of Dhanika*. Satyabhamabai Pandurang.

Dīkṣita, Appayya. 1903. *Kuvalayānanda*, edited by P.R. Subramanya Sharma. Banarjee Press.

Eagleton, Terry. 1996. *Literary Theory: An Introduction.* UK: Blackwell Publishers.

———. 2012. 'Doxa and Common Life: An Interview'. In *Mapping Ideology*, by Terry Eagleton, 265–277. Verso.

Eco, Umberto. 1995. 'Travels in Hyperreality'. In *Faith in Fakes*, 3–57. Vintage Books.

Edgerton, Franklin. 1953. *Buddhist Hybrid Sanskrit Grammar and Dictionary.* Vol. 1: Grammar. Yale University Press.

Eichenbaum, B.M. 1971. 'The Theory of the Formal Method'. In *Readings in Russian Poetics: Formalist and Structuralist Views*, edited by L. Matejka and K. Pomorska, 3–37. Michigan Slavic Publication.

Engels, Friedrich and Karl Marx. 2005. 'The Communist Manifesto by Friedrich Engels and Karl Marx'. Project Gutenberg, 25 January. Available at: www.gutenberg.org/ebooks/61, accessed on 15 September 2023.

Fish, Stanley. 1980. *Is There a Text in the Class: The Authority of Interpretive Communities.* Harvard University Press.

Foucault, Michael. 1972. 'Defining the Statement'. In *The Archeology of Knowledge*, 79–87. Pantheon Books.

———. 1980. 'Truth and Power'. In *Power Knowledge Selected Interviews and Other Writings 1972–1977*, edited by Colin Gordon and translated by Colin Gordon, Leo Marshall and Kate Soper, 109–133. Pantheon Books.

Freeman, Rich. 2003. 'Genre and Society: The Literary Culture of Premodern Kerala'. In *Literary Cultures in History: Reconstructions from South Asia*, edited by Sheldon Pollock, 437–502. University of California Press.

Gautama. 1913. *The Nyāyasūtra*, edited by B.D. Basu and translated by Satisha Vidyabhushana Chandra. The Panini Office.

George, K.M. 1973. 'Literary Criticism in Malayalam'. *Indian Literature*, 16 (3).

Gerow, Edwin. 1977. *Indian Poetics (A History of Indian Literature)*. Wiesbaden: Harrassowitz.

Gilles, D. and F. Guattari. 2005. *A Thousand Plateaus*, translated by B. Massumi. University of Minnesota Press.

Gramsci, Antonio. 2000. 'Intellectuals and Education'. In *Gramsci Reader*, edited by David Forgacs, 300–322. New York University Press.

Greenblatt, Stephen. 1980. *Renaissance Self-fashioning: From More to Shakespeare*. The University of Chicago Press.

Harré, Rom. 2002. *Cognitive Science: A Philosophical Introduction*. Sage.

Harrison, Bernard. 1991. *Inconvenient Fictions: Literature and the Limits of Theory*. Yale University Press.

Hedge, Suryanarayana. 2009. *The Concept of Vakrokti in Sanskrit Poetics*. Readworthy Publications.

Hemacandra. 1964. *Kāvyānuśāsana*, edited by R.C. Parikh and V.M. Kulkarni. Sri Mahavira Jaina Vidyalaya.

———. 2017. *Kāvyānuśāsana*, edited by Rasiklal C. Parikh. Bombay: Mahavira Jaina Vidyalaya.

Ingalls, Daniel H.H. 1990. 'Introduction'. In *Dhvanyāloka*, by Ānandavardhana, 1–39. Harvard University Press.

Jagannātha. 1888. *The Rasagaṅgādhara of Jagannātha Paṇḍita with the commentary of Nāgeśa Bhaṭṭa*. Edited by D. Prasad and K.P. Parab. Bombay: The Nirnaya Sagara Press.

Jaimini. 1923. *The Mimāmsasūtra*, edited by M.D. Basu. The Panini Office.

Jauss, Hans Robert. 1982. *Toward an Aesthetic of Reception*. University of Minnesota Press.

Jayadeva. 1932. *Chandrāloka of Shri Jayadēva with the Rākagāma Commentary by Gāgā Bhatta*, edited by Ananta Shasthri Vetal. Benares: Chowkamba Sanskrit Series Office.

Joshi, Ramlal and Digesh Mehta. 1985. 'An Essay from "Vivechanni Prakriya": The Critical Process'. *Indian Literature*, 28 (5): 48–52.

Joshi, Umashankar. 2017. 'The Relevance of Sanskrit Poetics to Contemporary Practical Criticism'. In *A Student's Handbook*, edited by Neeraja A. Gupta, 77–86. Cambridge Scholars.

Kalhaṇa. 1900. *Kalhaṇas Rājataraṅgiṇī: A Chronicle of the Kings of Kashmir*. Translated by M.A. Stein. Archibald Constable and Company.

Kavirāja. 1897. *Raghavapāṇḍaviya*, edited by Pandit Sivadatta. Nirnaya Sagar Press.

———. 1965. *Rāghavapāṇḍavīya of Kavirāja*, with commentary by Damodar Jha. Chowkhamba Vidyabhawan.

Keown, Damien. 2004. *A Dictionary of Buddhism*. Oxford University Press.

Krishnamoorthy, K. 1964. *Essays in Sanskrit Criticism*. Karnataka University.

———. 1977. 'Introduction'. In *Vakroktijīvita*. Dharwar University Press.

———. 2017. 'The Relevance of Rasa Theory to Modern Literature'. In *A Student's Handbook*, edited by Neeraja A. Gupta, 98–112. Cambridge Scholars.

Kṣemendra. 1954. *Aucityavicaracarcā*. In *Kṣemendra Studies: Together with an English Translation of his Kavikanthabharana, Aucityavicaracarca and Suvrttatilaka*, edited by Suryakanta, 118–172. Oriental Book Agency.

Kumārilabhaṭṭa. 1920. *Tantravārttika*. Ananda Sarma Sanskrit Series.

Kuntaka. 1977. *Vakroktijīvita*. Translated by K. Krishnamoorthy. Karnatak University.

———. 2009. *Vakroktijīvita*. Vallathol Vidyapitham.

Kushwaha, M.S. 1992. 'The Contemporary Relevance of Indian Aesthetics: Some Reflections'. *Journal of Comparative Literature and Aesthetics*, 15 (1–2): 110–113.

Lariviere, Richard W. 1980. 'The Vakrokti-jīvita of Kuntaka; Critically Edited with Variants, Introduction'. *Journal of the American Oriental Society*, 100 (3): 324.

Lessa, Iara. 2006. 'Discursive Struggles Within Social Welfare: Restaging Teen Motherhood'. *British Journal of Social Work*, 36 (2): 283–298.

Lienhard, Siegfried. 1984. *A History of Classical Poetry Sanskrit-Pali-Prakrit*. Otto Harrassowits.

Līlātilakam, ed. 1969. Kunchanpillai, Elamkulam. N.B.S.

Macaulay, T.B. 2015. 'Minute, dated the 2nd February 1835'. *Islamic Studies*, 54 (3/4): 237–248. Available at: http://www.jstor.org/stable/26393680, accessed on 7 September 2023.

Mahimabhaṭṭa. 1901. *Vyaktiviveka*, edited by T. Gaṇapati Śāstrī. Trivandrum Sanskrit Series.

Mammaṭa. 1966. *Kāvyaprakāśa of Mammaṭa*. Edited by Ganganath Jha. Varanasi: Bharathiya Vidya Prakashan.

Man, Paul de. 1996. *Blindness and Insight: Essays in the Rhetoric of Contemporary Criticism*. Routledge.

Māṇkha. 1984. *Sāhityamīmāṃsā*, edited by Gopinath Sastri. Varanasi: Sampurnanand Sanskrit University.

Misra, Ramachandra. 1998. *The Integral Advaitism of Sri Aurobindo*. Motilal Banarsidass Publishers.

Mukarovsky. 1964. 'Standard Language and Poetic Language'. In *A Prague School Reader on Esthetics, Literary Structure, and Style*, edited by P.L. Garvin, 17–30. George Town University Press.

Muller, F. Max, ed. 1884. 'Maitreya Upanishad'. In *The Upanishads Part II*, 285–346. Oxford.

Nagaraj, D.R. 2003. 'Critical Tensions in the History of Kannada Literary Culture'. In *Literary Cultures in History: Reconstructions from South Asia*, edited by Sheldon Pollock, 323–382. University of California Press.

Nye, Joseph S. 2010. 'The Future of Soft Power in US Foreign Policy.' *Soft Power and US Foreign Policy*, 216–23. Routledge.

Pandey, K.C. 2008. *Comparative Aesthetics*, Vol. I. Chowkamba Sanskrit Series.

Paniker, K. Ayyappa. 1999. 'Rasasidhānta navīkaraṇam'. In *Indian Sahitya Sidhantam Prasaktiyum Sadhyatayum*, 12–28. Bhasha Institute.

———. 2017. *K. Ayyappa Paniker: Selected Essays*. Edited by K. Satchidanandan. Sahitya Akademi.

Patañjali. 1986. *Patanjali's Vyakarana-Mahabhāsya*. Edited by S.D. Joshi and J.A.F. Roodbergen. University of Pune.

Patankar, R. 2017. 'Does the Rasa Theory Have Modern Relevance?' In *Student's Handbook of Indian Aesthetics*, edited by Neeraja A. Gupta, B.87–98. Cambridge Scholars.

Pathak, R.S. 1982. 'The Indian Theory of Vakrokti in Relation to the Stylistic Concept of Deviance'. *Annals of the Bhandarkar Oriental Research Institute*, 63 (1): 195–211.

Pollock, Sheldon. 1985. 'The Theory of Practice and the Practice of Theory in Indian Intellectual History'. *Journal of the American Oriental Society*, 105 (3): 499–519.

———. 2000. 'Indian Knowledge Systems on the Eve of Colonialism'. *Intellectual History Newsletter*, 22: 1–16.

———. 2001. 'New Intellectuals'. *The Indian Economic and Social History Review*, 38 (1): 3–31.

Pollock, Sheldon. 2001. 'The Social Aesthetic and Sanskrit Literary Theory'. *Journal of Indian Philosophy*, 29 (2): 197–229.

———. 2003. 'Sanskrit Literary Culture from the Inside Out'. In *Literary Cultures in History: Reconstructions from South Asia*. London: University of California Press.

———. 2006. *The Language of the Gods in the World of Men: Sanskrit, Culture and Power in Premodern India*. Los Angeles: Columbia University Press.

———. 2016. *The Rasa Reader*. Columbia University Press.

Pratihārendurāja. 1982. *Kāvyālaṇkara-sāra-saṇgraha with the commentary, the Laghuvrtti of Induraja*, edited by Narayana Daso Banhatti.Bhandarkar Oriental Research Institute.

Purohita, Devaśaṅkara. 1940. *Alaṅkāramanjuṣā*. Oriental Manuscript Library, Ujjain.

Raghavan, V. 1942. 'Aucitya'. In *Some Concepts of Alaṅkāraśāstra*. The Adayar Library.

Raja, Kunjunni. 2000. *Indian Theories of Meaning*. The Theosophical Society of India.

Rajan, R.S. 1986. 'After "Orientalism": Colonialism and English Literary Studies in India'. *Social Scientist*, 14 (7): 23–35. Available at: https://doi.org/10.2307/3517248, accessed on 20 September 2023.

Rājaśekhara. 1988. *The Burning Bush*. D.K. Publishers Distributors.

———. 2000. *Kāvyamīmāṃsā*. Edited by Sadhana Parashar. Delhi: D.K. Print World.

Rayan, Krishna. 1965. 'Rasa and the Objective Correlative'. *The British Journal of Aesthetics*, 5 (3): 246–260.

———. 2002. 'Rasa-dhvani Approach and Present Day Literary Criticism'. In *The Lamp and the Light*, edited by Krishna S. Arjunwadkar, 1–29. Sahitya Akademi.

Royle, N. 2003. *The Uncanny*. Manchester University Press.

Rudraṭa. 1886. *Kāvyalaṅkāra*. Nirnaya Sagar Press.

Ruyyaka. 1939. *Alaṅkārasarvasva*. Nirnaya Sagar Press.

Śabarasvāmin. 1923. *Śabarabhāṣya*, translated by Ganganath Jha, Vol. 1. Oriental Institute.

Śālikanātha. 1903. *Vākyarthamatravṛtti in Prakaranapañcika*, edited by H. Gupta. Chowkhamba Sanskrit Series.

Salomon, Richard. 1965. 'Rasa and the Objective Correlative'. *The British Journal of Aesthetics*, 5 (3): 246–260.

———. 1998. *Indian Epigraphy.* Oxford University Press.

Samudrabandha. 1915. *Alaṅkārasarvasva of Rājānaka Ruyyaka with the Commentary of Samudrabandha*, edited by Ganapathy Sastri. Travancore Government Press.

Śaṅkara. 1890. *Vedāntasūtra*. Clarendon Press.

Sastri, P.S. 1988. 'Indian Poetics and New Criticism'. In *Indian Poetics and Western Thought*. Argo Publishing House.

Sastri, S. Kuppuswamy. 1945. *Highways and Byways of Literary Criticism in Sanskrit*. Kuppuswamy Research Institute.

Satchidanandan, K. 2014. 'Dilemmas of Indian Literary Criticism'. *Frontline*, 21 March. Available at: https://frontline.thehindu.com/columns/K_Satchidanandan/dilemmas-of-indian-literary-criticism/article5739887.ece, accessed on 20 September 2023.

Saussure, Ferdinand de. 1959. *Course in General Linguistics*, edited by Charles Balley and Albert Sechehaye. Philosophical Society.

Shakespeare, William. 1918. *King Lear.* James M. Nixon, ESQ.

Shankara. 1890. *The Vedanta Sutra with the Commentary of Shankaracharya.* Oxford.

Shastry, P.S. 1988. 'Indian Poetics and New Criticism'. In *Indian Poetics and Western Thought*. Argo Publishing House.

Shklovsky, V. 1965. 'Art as Technique'. In *Russian Formalist Criticism: Four Essays*, edited by L.T. Lemon and M.J. Reis, 3–24. University of Nebraska Press.

Singh, Upinder. 2009. *A History of Ancient and Early Medieval India: From the Stone Age to the 12th Century.* Delhi: Pearson-Longman.

Sivarudrappa, G. S. and S.L. Seshagiri Rao. 1985. 'An Essay from "Kavyartha Chintana": Literary Criticism in Indian Poetics'. *Indian Literature*, 28 (5): 67–78.

Sreejan, V.C. 1999. *Arthantaranyasam.* Current Books.

Sreenath, V.S. 2019. 'Symbolic Power of Poetry'. *Economic and Political Weekly*, 54 (2): 70–71.

———. 2022. 'The Dhārmic Function of Sanskrit *Kāvya*: Poetry as a Suggestive Force'. *Journal of Dharma Studies*, 5 (2): 167–184.

Sreenath, V.S. and Mini Chandran. 2022. 'To Write Was to Cense Kāvyaśāstra and Creative Freedom in Premodern India'. *Economic and Political Weekly*, 57 (34).

Thapar, Romila. 2000. *History and Beyond: Interpreting Early India, Time as Metaphor of History, Cultural Transaction and Early India, From Lineage to State*. Oxford University.

———. 2002. *History of Early India from Origins to A.D. 1300*. New Delhi: Penguin.

Udbhaṭa. 1982. *Kāvyālaṅkāra-sāra-saṅgraha with the Commentary, the Laghuvrtti of Induraja*, edited by Narayana Daso Banhatti. Bhandarkar Oriental Research Institute.

Upadhyaya, Gangesa. 1901. *The Tattvacintāmaṇi*. Bibliotheca Indica.

Vāgbhaṭa II. 1915. *Kāvyānuśāsana*. Nirnaya Sagar Press.

Vālmīki. 2000. Available at: valmiki.iitk.ac.in., accessed in December 2017.

Vāmana. 2000. *Kāvyālaṅkārasūtravṛtti*. Kerala Bhasha Institute.

Vātsyāyana. 1896. *The Nyayasutras with Vatsyayana's Bhashya and Extracts from the Nyayavarttika and the Tatparyatika*, edited by Gangadhara Sastri Tailanga. E.J. Lazarus & Co.

Veluthat, Keshavan. 2013. 'Of Ubiquitous Heroines and Elusive Heros: The Cultural Milieu of Medieval *Maṇipravāḷa Kāvya*s from Kerala'. Indian Council of Historical Research.

Vidyānātha. 1933. *Pratāparudrīya*, edited by K.S. Ramamurthi and S.R. Matha. Oriental Research Institute.

Vijayavardhana, G. 2010. *Outlines of Sanskrit Poetics*. Chowkamba Sanskrit Series.

Viśvanātha. 2016. *Sāhityadarpaṇa*, translated by J.R. Ballantyne and Pramada Dasa Mitra. Motilal Banarsidas Publishers.

Viśveśvara. 1997. *Camatkāracandrikā*. Bharatiya Book Corporation.

Index

About the Author

Sreenath V.S. is Assistant Professor at the Department of Humanities and Social Sciences at IISER, Bhopal. He is the co-author, along with Professor Mini Chandran, of *An Introduction to Indian Aesthetics: History, Theory and Theoreticians*. He is also one of the editors of the volume titled *Aesthetics in India: Transitions and Transformations*. His scholarly pursuits encompass a range of areas, including Sanskrit literary theory and literature, colonial modernity, classical Malayalam literature, and the history of ideas. Additionally, Sreenath V.S. has received the prestigious Meenakshi Mukherjee Memorial Prize established by the Indian Association for Commonwealth Literature and Language Studies for his article 'What to Do with the Past?: Sanskrit Literary Criticism in Postcolonial Space'.